CALEDON SHIPS

A selection of Caledon built ships from the Dundee City Archives Collection

David E S Middleton
BSc MSc CEng FIMechE

D1421708

Friends of Dundee City Archives 2008

In memory of Jerry Wright

ISBN 978-0-9536553-7-3.

Published by the Friends of Dundee City Archives

Printed by Book Printing UK Peterborough

Acknowledgements

The author wishes to thank those who assisted in the preparation of this work and the following in particular:
Florence, Edward, Caroline and Fiona for their advice and assistance.
The staff of Dundee City Archives: Iain Flett, Richard Cullen and Angela Lockie.
The staff of Wellgate Library Dundee, Local Studies Dept. Dundee City Council.
The staff of University of Dundee Archives .
Jack Reilly one of the last Caledon Managers.

Fellow members of the Friends of Dundee City Archives.

Illustrations

Unless otherwise noted images are sourced from Dundee City Archives.
Unless otherwise mentioned the photographic images are reproduced with the permission of Marine Design Consultants Ltd courtesy of Dundee City Archives.
The images were commissioned by the Caledon S&E Co. largely from local professional photographers including Norman G Brown and J D Forbes.
The images of ships: AGAMEMNON, BACCHUS, HESPERUS, ABERTAY and PLOVER and workers of ASCOT and HERON are © The Courier D C Thompson & Co Ltd and are included by courtesy of The Courier D C Thomson & Co Ltd. .

The frontispiece colour image is of the painting by Robert Lloyd of the Blue Funnel Line ship "MV DIOMED at Hong Kong" reproduced with the kind permission of the artist. This image exists in the Archive on a Christmas card from The Blue Funnel Line.

The author was a Caledon Marine Engineering apprentice in the late 1950's, the ships encountered being DIOMED to ATHELPRINCESS, before going on to experience other areas of Mechanical Engineering and study the subject at undergraduate and postgraduate level at Strathclyde and Birmingham Universities.
His career included posts at BP Chemicals at Grangemouth, The National Engineering Laboratory East Kilbride and the University of Dundee.

"Far away places with strange sounding names"

MV DIOMED at Hong Kong by Robert Lloyd

MV DIOMED was built at the Caledon Shipyard Dundee in 1956 for the Blue Funnel Line
This painting embodies the atmosphere of romance, spirit of adventure and foreign travel imagined by many a young person anticipating a career in the Merchant Navy.

Introduction

The Caledon Shipbuilding and Engineering Company Dundee Scotland

The Caledon company was established by W. B. Thompson who opened the Tay Foundry at Stobswell Dundee in 1866 where four steam powered yachts were built before the Caledon yard was established at the shore in Dundee on the North bank of the River Tay. Ship No.6 was the yacht BANSHEE for the earl of Caledon after whom the yard was named. The firm traded as W.B. Thompson until 1896 when prevailing conditions caused a re-formation of the company under the new name of Caledon Shipbuilding and Engineering Company.

The shipyard by 1916 was situated at Carolina Port and the Marine Engine works, taken over by W.B. Thompson in 1889, were at Lilybank Foundry bounded by Kemback St, Arbroath Road and Morgan St. In 1916 a boilershop and 130 ton crane were built at Carolina Port and a new shipyard laid down at Stannergate.

The Lilybank engine works survived in production till 1932 when the last engine, for the KYLECLARE, was produced. This occurred when the UK shipbuilding industry was in depression. It is worth noting that much of the content of a Caledon built ship was sourced in Scotland from the engines, boilers, pumps and steering gear to the majority of the steel and fastenings.

Shipbuilding in the UK faced increasing world competition in the 1960's and large scale rationalisation took place resulting in the Caledon company joining Henry Robb of Leith to become Robb Caledon in 1968. The last vessels at the Caledon Shipyard were built in 1980.

During the life of the yard 509 ships were built with 20 barges and 34 launches in addition.

Caledon built ships gained a reputation for quality and longevity which was rewarded by repeat business over many decades from top drawer merchant shipping companies.

This work aims to stand witness to the management, design and workmanship which sustained the company through more than a century of high quality shipbuilding.

The Case Studies included in this publication.

The presentation of the case studies is in Ship No. order which is roughly chronological.

The photographs and supporting notes are generally based on those available in the Dundee City Archives with a few exceptions.

Where multiple identical designs are involved only one example is normally included. There was only one existing photographic example found before the formation of the Caledon company in 1896 but earlier images may survive in other collections.

General dimensions, propulsion details etc. are given where known but there are a few exceptions where no data (nd) were found.

Data Format

Unless otherwise stated the ship's main engines were manufactured by Lilybank Foundry as either W. B. Thompson or Caledon Shipbuilding & Engineering Co.

In multi expansion engines the first numbers are cylinder diameters in inches with stroke after the oblique sign e.g. 12 18 30/20.

Main boiler pressure is given as HP in pounds per square inch.

Tonnage is quoted as Gross Registered for Merchant ships and Standard displacement for Naval ships.

Abbreviations

ctl	Constructive total loss	PS	Paddle steamer
L/V	Light vessel	SS	Single Screw Steamship
L/H	Light house	TSS	Twin Screw steamship
LR	Lloyds Register	MV	Motor Vessel
nd	No data available	TSMV	Twin screw motor vessel
DEMS	Defensively equipped Merchant Ship		

References

[1] Ingram papers, Local Studies, Dundee City Council library Wellgate and University of Dundee Archives.

[2] Caledon papers, City of Dundee Archives.

[3] Newspaper cuttings, Dundee City Library Local Studies collection.

[4] Caledon papers City of Dundee Archives generally GD324/5/4/7.

[5] Drummond C. "The Remarkable Life of Victoria Drummond Marine Engineer" Pub I.Mar.E. 1994

[6] Caledon Ships database, by Norman Smith, Dundee City Archives.

[DM] Author

Dundee City Archives photographs are generally from Ref: GD324/6/3/xx/yy.

An index of ships included is at page 161.

SS FINGAL

SS FINGAL was built for the London and Edinburgh shipping Co. of Leith for the carriage of 200 passengers. (The engine power for this ship size was very high but this was presumably to beat the competition just as the railways were doing about this time.[DM])

It was a great initial success and was built to beat the Carron ships on the Leith to London service. She made Leith from Gravesend in 23hrs 25min on June 21st 1894 making it the fastest ship on the East coast.

Three men suffocated while working a cargo of Guano at Leith 6/5/1904. Damaged in collision with the Dundee built BATAVIER in the Thames in December 1905.

Torpedoed by U-23 [6], while on trip from London to Leith with general cargo, off Coquet Island (Northumberland) March 15 1915. Six of crew of 28 lost. The starboard boat was dragged down with ship.[1]

Built 1894　　　　　Yard No 121

Specifications
1548 Gross tons
280 x 35x 18 feet

Machinery Engine No 250
Steam   Triple expansion 4652 IHP
32 49 80/48　　HP 175psi
17 knots

Complement
120 Passengers　nd Crew　[4]

SS SALMO

Dundee City Archives

SS SALMO was built for Thomas Wilson & Co of Hull for the carriage of 120 passengers.
In 1914 she took 261 stevedores from London to Rouen to unload transports. They slept between the hatches. There was trouble aboard at Rouen and eventually all were sent home.
Aground ex Stavanger for Hull 1902.
Torpedoed 17/4/1917 210 miles NW of Fastnet on passage from Oporto to Liverpool[6] with the loss of three lives.[1]

Built 1900   Yard No 152

Specifications
1722 Gross tons
265 x 35x 16 feet

Machinery   Engine No 290
Steam Triple Expansion   1770 IHP
21.5 36 52/36   HP 200 psi
13 knots

Complement
120 Passengers   nd Crew

SS CALIFORNIAN

Courtesy of US National Archive ARC 278339 (Photo taken from CARPATHIA 14/5/1912)

SS Californian was built for the Leyland Line of Liverpool for the carriage of 60 passengers and cargo on the trans-Atlantic route to North America.

While ordered for the Leyland line it was to be managed by J R Ellerman but was delivered to a USA syndicate led by J Pierpoint Morgan.

Transport of engines and boilers overnight from Lilybank foundry to Victoria dock was a spectacle and many thousands stayed up to see the traction engines at work.

The heaviest loads were the two 85 ton boilers on 20 ton bogies. Much damage was caused to drain covers and services. One boiler sank into the road in Meadowside and stuck there overnight.

The Master was accused of not responding to TITANIC's distress signals five miles away.

The solitary radio operator was off duty at the time. Rockets were seen but disaster was not suspected. At the TITANIC disaster inquest Lord Mersey said that the CALIFORNIAN could have forced its way through the ice to save lives.

Took fire at Vera Cruz 2/7/1913 with serious damage by fire and water.

Torpedoed by U-34 and damaged. Was under tow when torpedoed again by U-35 [6] and sunk off Cape Matapan, Peloponnese Greece 10/11/1915. [1]

Built 1901	Yard No 159
Specifications 6223 Gross tons 447 x 54 x 30 feet	
Machinery Steam Triple Expansion 3072 IHP 26 43.5 74/60	Engine No 299 HP 200psi
Complement 60 Passengers nd Crew	

SS Kurgan

SS KURGAN was built for Danish owners but purchased on the stocks by Messrs Kurgan of St Petersburg for £50,000. It had refrigerated space. Launched without name and no public were allowed in the yard. In collision off Gravesend October 4th 1910 with the Glasgow ship LADY GERTRUDE COCHRANE at anchor. By 1910 owned by Handelshaus Bros Lassman of Lindau Russia. Employed in the London –St Petersburg service carrying perishable cargo and passengers. In 1914 owned by Helmsing and Grimm of Riga. Renamed CESAREWICH ALEXIJ [1]. Sunk by U Boat U-60 on 29/7/1917 15miles East of Lerwick while on passage from Archangel to Liverpool [6].

Built 1903	Yard No 171
Specifications 2387 Gross tons 290 x 40 x 20 feet	
Machinery Steam Triple Expansion 21.5 36 62/45	Engine No 308 2550 IHP HP 200 psi

SS SELANGOR

The first Caledon built ship for the Straits Steamship Co. and employed for the carriage of passengers and cargo on the Singapore to Port Swettenham and Penang route.
Scrapped in 1934 at Singapore.[1]
Port of registry Singapore. Contract price £21,000. Arrived at Singapore in December 1903. In 1902 C.W. Laird retired and was replaced by D.K. Somerville who had previous maritime experience operating steam packets out of Belfast and who adapted the Straits Steamship fleet to operate in a similar manner. Passenger numbers rose and he realized the fleet was dated so he ordered new tonnage from Dundee. Straits Times said "She was undoubtedly the best equipped and most comfortable of all passenger vessels among the local shipping. She made the voyage from Dundee in 35 days at an average speed of 11 knots. She will take the place of MALLACA next week on the run up the Straits to Port Swettenham and Penang" .[2]

Built 1903   Yard No 173

Specifications
1019 Gross tons
225 x 34x 14 feet

Machinery   Engine No 312
Steam Triple expansion   1413 IHP
20 33 54/36   HP 185 psi
11 knots

Complement
50 1st Class Passengers   nd Crew

SS GRIVE

SS GRIVE was built for the General Steam Navigation Co of London for the London, Southampton and Bordeaux service.
Damaged in collision during a storm with the French ship SS SOUTENNES at Bordeaux 22/4/1914. Sank the barge MARGARET in collision in the Thames 17/1/1906. In collision with SS CHARLES de BELGIQUE off Wapping 21/1/1908.
At the Coronation Review Spithead June 1911. Armed as a boarding steamer in the White Sea Patrol in the Great War. Torpedoed off Lerwick 8/12/1917 by German Submarine UC-40 and later foundered 23/12/1917. [1] [6].

Built 1905   Yard No 179

Specifications
2038 Gross tons
291 x 41 x 20 feet

Machinery   Engine No 318
Steam Triple Expansion   2154 HP
24.5 39 64/45   HP 170psi

SS KINTA

SS KINTA was built for Straits Steamship Co of Singapore for the carriage of 108 passengers and cargo. Bombed and Sunk 1942. Scrapped in1946 at Singapore [1].
She sailed from Singapore in damaged condition having been dive bombed by Japanese in the Malacca Straits.(1942). Sunk by Japanese in Batavia and abandoned as beyond repair. Salvaged by the Japanese and used for the remainder of hostilities until surrender. In 1945 returned to owners in Singapore but judged to be beyond repair and broken up in 1946 [6].

Built 1907   Yard No 196

Specifications
1220 Gross tons
244 x 35x 15 feet

Machinery   Engine No 336
Steam Triple Expansion   1759HP
20.75 33 64/36   HP 185 psi
14.5 knots

Complement
108 Passengers   nd Crew

TSY TRIAD

TSY TRIAD was the first substantial order after a quiet spell. and was a private steam yacht for a Mr Shenley. The dining room, drawing room and owner's private accommodation was as far as possible a replica of Mr Shenley's private residence. A searchlight was fitted, a steam launch capable of 17 knots, a motor launch capable of 27 knots and another motor boat. Refitted at Dundee in 1911. Sold to a Richard Grech of Constantinople in September 1912. Bought by the Admiralty in 1915 and used as the HQ ship at the Dardanelles campaign. In 1929 was the senior naval Officer's yacht in the Persian Gulf. She was of 2354 tons had 2 funnels, 4x 3pounder guns and was capable of 14 knots.[1]

Engined by Builders; Contract Price being costs plus 5% Profit
Used by the Turkish Navy. In 1915 Bought by Admiralty for £40,000; H.Q.Ship at Dardanelles
1919 Served as Senior Naval Officer Headquarters, Persian Gulf
1933 Sold at Bombay.[6]

The White ensign was flown at her launch. Members of The Royal Yacht Squadron, an exclusive sailing club based on the isle of Wight, are permitted to fly this flag.[DM]

Built 1909	Yard No 194
Specifications 1182 Gross tons 250 x 35x 19 feet	
Machinery Steam Triple expansion, twin 20 32.5 52.5/ 36 2 x 1800IHP est 14 knots	Engine No 340, 341 HP 180psi

SS NORNA

Built for Fisheries support duties. Trials at Aberlady attaining a speed of 12.6 knots. Broken up at Troon in 1960. [1]

Built 1909   Yard No 208

Specifications
457 Gross tons
150 x 25x 14 feet

Machinery   Engine No 355
Steam Triple expansion 900 IHP
14 23 38/27   HP 185 psi
12 knots
(After ship No 209 Engine-No is Ship-No plus 200)

Complement
 4-1st class passengers   21 Crew

SS NORWEGIAN

SS NORWEGIAN was built for the Leyland Line of Liverpool for the transport of general cargo. Severely damaged by enemy action, mine or torpedo, off Seven Heads Southern Ireland 13/3/1917 while bound for New York from Liverpool. Beached off Galley Head but salvage of hull impracticable. Sixty ingots of Nickel were salved from cargo October 1920 and forwarded to Liverpool[1] .

SS NORWEGIAN (2) A second identical ship of the same name was built in 1920; probably a replacement vessel for the war loss she ran trials on 25th Aug 1921.[DM]

1934 sold to Donaldson Line Ltd.; Donaldson Bros.Ltd., Managers; Registry unchanged – Liverpool. 1954 sold to CIA. de Navegacion Admirante A.A. Panama; renamed MARIA ELAINE Port of Registry Panama. 1959 sold to Japanese Shipbreakers; arrived at Osaka to be broken up.[6]

.

Built 1913   Yard No 234

Specifications
6357 Gross tons
400 x 52x 29 feet

Machinery   Engine No 434
Steam Quadruple Expansion   2750 IHP
23.5 34 49 70/51   HP 215 psi
10 knots

Complement
 15 1st class passengers   60 Crew

SS FORMBY

Dundee City Archives

SS FORMBY was built for the Clyde shipping Co of Glasgow for passenger and cattle transport in the Irish Sea service. It accommodated 39 cabin plus steerage passengers with a certificate for a total of 120 passengers and crew. She was sunk in 1917 by submarine U-62 in Caernarvon bay after leaving Liverpool for Waterford. Loss of fifteen lives (all hands) including master.[1]

Built 1914   Yard No 238

Specifications
1282 Gross tons
270 x 36x 17 feet

Machinery
Steam Triple expansion 2889 IHP
26 42 70/42   HP 180 psi
14 knots

Complement
 120 Passengers and 15 Crew

SS MACHAON

SS MACHAON is shown alongside the Boilershop fitting out wharf at Carolina Port. The then new 130 ton crane is seen to the South of the also new Boilershop building and the old Caledon yard is to the West (left) of the Boilershop. At the time of her launch the yard had 4,000 employees and the weekly wage bill was £14,000.[1]

The ship was built for the Ocean Steamship Co, managers Alfred Holt & Co Liverpool, with original accommodation for 6 first class and 36 steerage class passengers. The vessel could be fitted out to carry 450 passengers when on pilgrim voyages to Jeddah .[2]

In 1935 transferred to Glen Line and renamed GLENAFFRIC; in 1947 reverted to Ocean SS Co and renamed MACHAON; in 1950 transferred to Glen Line and renamed GLENAFFRIC; in 1950 sold for scrap for £55,000 and broken up at Briton Ferry Breakers (Thos. Ward) in South Wales .[6]

Caledon engine book gives engine power as 5134IHP. Was this a case of the design power not being achieved on trial?[DM]

Built 1916   **Yard No** 252

Specifications
7806 Gross tons
452 x 56 x 35 feet

Machinery
Steam   Triple expansion 4800 IHP
31 51.5 86/60   HP 195 psi
14 knots

Complement
42 Passengers   89 Crew

SS TUSKAR

SS TUSKAR was built for the Clyde Shipping Co Glasgow. Engaged in the cattle trade on the Waterford to Liverpool service with capacity for 500 animals.
Trial Trip Speed 14.50 knots, crew 30.
Sold in 1937 to Capt. Eric Ericson of Sweden and renamed LOLA. Port of Registry Surte. Sunk at Thesalonika under the German flag 1944 [1].

Built 1920	**Yard No** 255

Specifications
1164 Gross tons
270 x 36 x 17 feet

Machinery
Steam Triple expansion 2700 IHP
26 42 70/42   HP 180
14.5 knots

Complement   30 Crew

TSMV TANTALUS

Dundee City Archives

TSMV TANTALUS was built for Alfred Holt Ltd (Blue Funnel Line).

The ship was near the Seychelles in November 1940 when the Brocklebank liner MONDESOR was sunk by the raider ATLANTIS. The MONDESOR SOS enabled TANTALUS to be diverted away from danger zone.

TANTALUS was at Hong Kong for refit when the threat of Japanese invasion was imminent. Much of the machinery was dismantled and it was obvious that she could not leave under her own power. The ship was put in dry dock for removal of her propellers. The main engine machinery was shipped aboard and stowed in a hold and 300 tons of coal was loaded for the accompanying tug KESWICK which was to tow her to Singapore. She left Hong Kong on December 5th and made barely 5 knots. Japan declared war on December 8th 1941 and British ships in dangerous waters were ordered to seek refuge. Captain R. O. Morris had TANTALUS taken in to Manila on December 11th. All ships were ordered to Western Australia via the Lambok Strait but this was out of the question for TANTALUS. Manila and the ships were bombed daily and though the ship returned with Ack-Ack fire it was ineffective due to the altitude of the bombers. On Christmas day two salvos fell close by and the ship was shaken but not hit. Captain Morris had the ship moved to Bataan to get the protection of the shore batteries there. On December 26th the loss of the ship was practically inevitable and the crew were taken ashore and reached Manila. Waves of bombers attacked and the ship was hit four times and set ablaze. TANTALUS sank at 5:40 pm.[1]

She was transferred to Glen Line in 1936 renamed RADNORSHIRE but returned to Ocean Steamship Co. in 1939 and reverted to TANTALUS.[6]

Built 1923   Yard No 278
Specifications
7776 Gross tons
452 x 58x 35 feet
Machinery
Burmeister &Wain Diesel   6000 BHP
8 cyl 740mm bore 1150mm stroke
13.2knots

Complement
nd Passengers   nd Crew
Fitted for Mecca pilgrims, 432 persons.

14

SS ROYAL FUSILIER

SS ROYAL FUSILIER was built for the London and Edinburgh Shipping Company.
She ran trials in Firth of Forth in 1924 attaining a speed of 14.87 knots.
Sunk in 1941 near May island after a German aircraft bombed and damaged the vessel near Alnmouth; taken in tow but capsized and sunk 2.4 miles NE of Bass Rock. On passage London to Leith with 50 tons rice and 70 tons paper.[1]

Built 1924   **Yard No** 285

Specifications
2186 Gross tons
290 x 41x 19 feet

Machinery
Steam Triple Expansion 3000 IHP
26 42 70/45   HP 180 psi
14.87 knots

Complement
149 1st Class, 130 2nd Class Passengers
 44 Crew

SS KHOEN HOED

SS KHOEN HOED was built for the Thong Steamship Co.(Managers Hendry Brothers London for Chinese Thong EK Steamship Co., Pontianak, Borneo) for the carriage of passengers and cargo. For service in the Straits of Mallaca between Singapore and Pontianak.

Sold to John Manners of Hong Kong for £95,000 in 1954. Scrapped 1955 [1].

Built 1924   Yard No 289

Specifications
1237 Gross tons
245 x 85x 12 feet

Machinery
Steam Triple expansion 850 IHP twin screw 12 20 33/23 manufactured by Wm. Beardmore Co Coatbridge.
11 knots

Complement
22 Passengers   44 Crew

FERRY WALLASEY

SS WALLASEY was built for the Wallasey Corporation to ferry passengers on the Wallasey – Liverpool route. The WALLASEY and its sister vessel MARLOWE when completed in 1927 represented a great design step forward for ferries operating on the river Mersey. New features introduced were the cruiser stern, twin Flettner rudders and a permanent wooden shelter over the after part of the promenade deck. The ferries could carry in excess of 2200 passengers and were mainly employed on the Liverpool to Seacombe service. At the end of WALLASEY 's service its bell was placed in a prominent position in Wallasey town hall. The ferry's wheel, engine room telegraph, the binnacle and two steam whistles were presented to Liverpool Corporation for preservation in the planned city maritime museum.

She was the oldest Mersey ferry when scrapped, at Ghent, and the last steamer.

She cost £42,298 and was in several collisions the worst being with the Swedish steamship ALIDA CARTHON July 22 1954 which also hit three tugs. Her superstructure was totally damaged and steering and engine telegraph were out of order. Sold for scrap for £5,150.[1]

Trial Trip 12th June 1927 Mean Speed 12.356 knots

Accommodation for 16 Crew Members B.of T. Passenger Certificate for 2233 persons.[6]

Built 1927   Yard No 306

Specifications
813 Gross tons
157 x 48x 14 feet

Machinery
Steam Triple expansion 1200 IHP
14.5 23.5 38/24   HP 180 psi
12 knots

Complement
2233 Passengers on a steam V Certificate
16 Crew

SS PORTSDOWN

SS PORTSDOWN was built for the Southern Railway Co. for the Portsmouth – Ryde ferry service. No sleeping quarters fitted.
She struck a submerged object after leaving Ryde for Portsmouth 14/9/32 putting the Engines out of order.
Commisioned in a hurry in June 1940 as HMS PORTSDOWN and left Sheerness commanded by Sub Lieut R H Church RNVR.[1]

Portsmouth-Ryde Service Passenger Certificate issued by B.O.T. 727 passengers Summer 611 Winter.
1940 June 1st-2nd At Dunkirk Beaches.
1941 Mined and sunk off Portsmouth whilst on Portsmouth-Ryde service; 20 lives lost and 17 lives saved.[6]

Built   1928   **Yard No** 320
Specifications
  341 Gross tons
  190 x 25 x 9 feet
Machinery
Steam Compound Diagonal Paddle
27 51 /54   HP 1050 IHP
by J. Inglis of Glasgow.
13.5 knots

Complement
  Passengers   BoT certificate for 727
summer and 611 winter.   14 Crew

SS WATFORD

Dundee City Archives

SS WATFORD was built for Watts Watts Co. Arranged for carriage of Grain in Bulk
On September 10th 1932 she was wrecked on Cape Breton Island whilst on passage from Montreal to Sidney [C.B]; back Broken and abandoned [6].
Fuel consumption stated to be 29 tons per day at 10 knots. [2]
(Why did Watts want a North Eastern Marine engine rather than a Lilybank engine, was it for better fuel economy?)[DM]
Sister ship to SS WENDOVER.

Built 1928   Yard No 322

Specifications
5421 Gross tons
405 x 54x 30 feet

Machinery
Steam   Triple expansion 2100 IHP by
North Eastern Marine Eng., Co., Wallsend
25.5 42 70/48   HP 185psi
12.3 knots

Complement
0 Passengers   42 Crew

19

Ferry B. L. NAIRN

The ferry B.L. Nairn was built for the Dundee Harbour Trust for the Dundee to Newport Tay river crossing to carry passengers and road vehicles.

(One of the engine frames was cracked while in service and since Lilybank Foundry had since closed and the pattern was not available a new frame was cast by using the cracked frame as a pattern. It was said that the impression of the crack could clearly be seen on the engine after the rebuild. This story was related to DM by a Caledon MED engineering journeyman fitter.)

Built 1929   Yard No 330

Specifications
395 Gross tons
161 x 31x 8 feet

Machinery
Steam 2 – sets diagonal compound paddle engines of total power 465 IHP by Lilybank . Engines could operate independently or coupled.
Cyls 18 34/42   HP 120 psi
Speed 9.5 knots

Complement
Passengers 780 winter, 1107 summer
Crew nd

TSMV MARON

The twin screw motor vessel TSMV MARON was built for the China Mutual Steam Navigation Co. with the Alfred Holt Co of Liverpool as managers.[2]

Fitted for the Carriage of Pilgrims travelling from the Far East to Mecca. Complement 70 persons steerage, cabin passengers 6; A Holt & Co., Managers.

Engined by North Eastern Marine Eng. Co., Ltd., Wallsend.

1930 Ran Trials off Auchmithie. Mean speed 15.51 knots.

1942 Torpedoed by U-73 off Oran Pos'n Lat 36'27'N. Long 00'58'W. [6]

At Hong Kong in1937 she was requisitioned to take 1100 soldiers of the Royal Welsh Fusiliers to Shanghai with accommodation between decks. Many 1000's of dollars landed for the HSBC (Hong Kong and Shanghai Banking Company). Invading Japanese were active near the city and MARON was shelled by Chinese batteries.

In September-October 1939 she helped transfer BEF and equipment to France.

October 1942 in convoy for the North African campaign. Torpedoed and sunk in 15 minutes November 13th 1942 off Arzew during the North Africa landings. The Crew of 93 were saved by RN vessel HMS MARIGOLD and landed at Gibraltar.[1]

Built 1929   Yard No 329

Specifications
6701 Gross tons
426 x 56 x 32 feet
Machinery
Diesel twin NEM 6 cyl 4 stroke single
acting 5500 BHP total
820 mm bore 1300 mm stroke
15.5 knots

Complement
76 Passengers   70 Crew

MV TANIMBAR

MV TANIMBAR was built for Maatshappi Nederland. Engined by Sulzer Bros.
Fitted for carriage of Pilgrims complement 69.
At Launch a strong ebb tide and gale force NW wind carried the vessel down river. Brought up to anchor off Tayport Light; berthed by two tugs on next tide.
In 1942 she was sunk by enemy air attacks in convoy sailing from the Clyde - Gibraltar to Malta, North of Bone, Algeria. Twenty three lives lost.[6]
In 1932 she took 31 days 3hrs on voyage from Sydney to Dunkirk which was a record minimum. Sunk in 1942 by Italian Savoia torpedo bombers. P&O liners BHUTAN and BURDWAH were sunk in same convoy.[1]

Built 1930   **Yard No** 332

Specifications
 8169 Gross tons
 465 x 62 x 36 feet

Machinery
Diesel Sulzer 8cyl 2 stroke 7000 BHP
820 mm bore 1440 mm stroke
Not fitted at Caledon
14 knots

Complement
69 Passengers   69 Crew

TSMV AGAMEMNON

© The Courier D C Thomson & Co Ltd

TSMV AGAMEMNON (or MEMNON) was built for the Ocean Steamship Co.; A.Holt & Co., Managers.
Fitted for Carriage of Pilgrims, 80 crew, 6-1st class 12 Steerage Passengers. Trial Trip Dundee to Glasgow.[2]
After leaving Freetown on July 9 1940 she intercepted a message from the French probably in Dakar ordering a
French submarine to intercept and attack a British ship probably in reprisal for the British Navy firing on the
French naval ships in Oran and Dakar. At 6pm at a position 50 miles North of Dakar a sub fired two torpedoes
but they passed astern. On October 8 1941 she was one of 4 vessels with a heavy escort which left Alex with
supplies for Malta. Italian Naval ships were warded off by escort.
She was lost homeward bound via the Cape on March 11 1941 200 miles West of Cape Blanco; torpedoed by
U-106, hit aft and sank quickly with the loss of 4 lives.
A Spanish ship 150 miles away answered the distress signal but no rescue was made.
Her boats made it to Gambia.[1]

Built 1930   Yard No 334

Specifications
7730 Gross tons
454 x 59x 35 feet

Machinery
Diesel, Engines supplied by Burmeister
& Wain, Copenhagen, total 8600 BHP
740 mm bore 1500 stroke
16 knots

Complement
18 Passengers   80 Crew

TSMV BRALANTA

The tanker TSMV BRALANTA was built for Aktiebolaget Gotaverken* of Sweden;
Redri A/S Freikall, Managers. (Sister ships SKOTAS, KALMIA, FOSNA, and THORDIS also built at Caledon
with similar engine fitting out arrangements.)
1931 Hull towed to Gothenburg by tug GANGES for Engine installation by the Gotaverken company.[2]
In 1936 sold to Larentens Skibs A/S Oslo; Re named JAMES STOVE Port of Registry Oslo.
1940 Torpedoed and sunk as JAMES STOVE in the Gulf of Aden, near Aden by Italian Submarine
GALILEO.[6]
The submarine was based at Massawa and was the first indication that Italian subs were operating from
Eritrea.[1]
* This company was founded in 1850 by a Dundonian named Alexander Keiller.

Built 1931   Yard No 336

Specifications
8215 Gross tons
450 x 59x 35 feet

Machinery
Diesel engines supplied and fitted in
Sweden, Gotaverken 7 cyl 4-stroke
total 3900 BHP 550mm bore 1000 mm
stroke
12.4 knots

Complement
  38 Crew

SS KYLECLARE

SS KYLECLARE was built for the Limerick Steamship Co. for the carriage of livestock.
This ship had the last main engine to be constructed at Lilybank foundry and Engine Works, 3 Kemback Street Dundee; she ran trials off the Tees.
Fitted for Livestock/ Capacity; Sheep only 2,171. or Cattle 238, Sheep 607 and horses 4.
1943 Torpedoed off Leixoes, Portugal by U456 while on passage Lisbon to Dublin. [6]
She was a shallow draft vessel and traded to Irish west Coast ports. In 1940 picked up crew of CLAN MENZIES which had been torpedoed off County Mayo.
Torpedoed and sunk 21/2/1943 with 18 lost while on passage from Lisbon to Dublin.[1]

Built 1932   **Yard No** 342

Specifications
699 Gross tons
210x 32 x 13 feet

Machinery
Steam   Triple expansion 950 IHP
17 28 46/33   HP 185psi
12 knots

Complement
15 Passengers   22 Crew

MV GORGON

MV GORGON was built for the Ocean S.S. Co. (Singapore -West Australian Ports service) ; managers Alfred Holt & Co. Liverpool. At launch the bottle failed to break and the ship was launched without ceremony. The ceremony was successfully completed later in the day with the ship alongside the fitting out jetty at the Boilershop.

At Singapore when the Japanese approached in 1942. She unloaded live sheep cargo but was ordered to leave with remaining cargo and, though desertions had depleted crew, made for Australia with 380 refugee passengers on board. Bombed from high and low level but reached Freemantle safely. Bombed at Milne Bay New Guinea from 200 feet and made for sea at full speed with all guns in action. One plane was hit and crashed another was hit and left; bombing caused fire on board. She reached Freemantle with 6 crew dead and 23 wounded. Towed to Cairns then Brisbane for repairs.[1]

She ran trials off Firth of Tay. Her hull was of specially strengthened design to lie aground in North Western Australian Ports such as Broome. Fitted for carriage of 550 cattle, Passengers 138 1st class and 24 2nd class. Complement 91 persons

In 1964 she was sold for £49,250 to Hong Kong breakers the Keung Yau Shipbuilding Co.[6]

Built 1933   **Yard No** 344

Specifications
3533 Gross tons
315 x 51x 24 feet

Machinery
Diesel 4000 BHP by B&W Copenhagen
2 stroke 6 cyl
450mm bore 1200 mm stroke
14 knots

Complement
162 Passengers   83 Crew

SS DUNDEE

Dundee City Archives

SS DUNDEE was built for the Dundee Perth and London Shipping Co. of Dundee (DP&L).
Tenders for construction were Caledon (Kincaid engine) £66,875, Caledon (Stephen engine) £66,965 {accepted}, Ailsa £67,450, Stephen £68,700, H&W Govan £70,000, Scotts £70,900. Severe stranding occurred at Green Scaup on the south side of the river off Monifieth in April 1935 and the ship was refloated after several days with the aid of tugs and the backwash off the Brocklebank liner STOCKWELL. Typical voyage in 1940 was coal from Grangemouth to Lisbon returning with cork Oporto to Kirkaldy. In 1943 it was one of 16 ships fitted out for convoy rescue work in the North Atlantic with crew of 84 officers and men.[1]
1945 Returned to Owners .1950 Converted to burn Oil Fuel.
1961 Sold for breaking up at Bilbao, by A.F.Ondas arrived at Bilbao 28/8/61.[6]

Built 1933   **Yard No** 345

Specifications
1540 Gross tons
281 x 42 x 17 feet

Machinery
Steam Triple expansion 1800 IHP supplied by A Stephen of Glasgow
20.5 35 59/42   HP 220 psi
12.5 knots

Complement
12 Passengers   32 Crew

MV ARBROATH

MV ARBROATH was built for the DP&L Co. of Dundee and was their first motor coaster. At the launch the bottle only broke at the third attempt.[1]
Engined by British Auxiliaries Ltd, Glasgow.
Shortly after delivery she was chartered to lay two telephone cables across River Tay which required voyage to Woolwich to load two cables; laying cables required two days.
In 1949 it was in collision with Finnish steamer AINA MARIA NORMINEN and was beached at Whitby, refloated and towed to Dundee for repairs by builders.
In 1962 she was sold to James Tyrell [of Arklow] Dublin for £20,000 and renamed VALZELL. Port of Registry Dublin.
In 1972 broken up by Haulbowline Industries Ltd.Co., Cork. [6]

Built 1935   **Yard No** 347

Specifications
553 Gross tons
165 x 30 x 14 feet

Machinery
Diesel Atlas Polar 500 BHP
350 bore 570 stroke
10.5 knots

Complement
0 Passengers   8 Crew

SS RATNAGIRI

Dundee City Archives

SS RATNAGIRI* was built for Indian owners the **Ratnagar Steamship Co., Messrs Hall, Angrer & Co., London Managers. At launch the bottle failed to break twice. This was a two funneled steamer with accommodation for 1200 deck passengers on the Bombay–Goa service. She was commandeered by the Royal Indian Navy in 1940 for the duration of the war. (Prior to fall of Keren and Asmara, Eritrea, she landed troops and supplies at difficult points on the coast. She returned to civil duties after WW2 and was used on passenger service between Bombay and Debhul with a capacity for 300. (Classed for Karachi-Mangalore Coastal Service).

Scrapped in 1966 at Bombay. (*Name is Hindustani for fast carriage). [1]
** Merged with Scindia Steam Navigation later.[Google books].
In 1966 Sold to Abid & Co., Bombay for breaking up for £14,286.[6]

Built 1935   **Yard No** 348

Specifications
606 Gross tons
210 x 35 x 11 feet

Machinery
Steam Triple expansion by McKee Baxter
of Govan   2000 IHP
13.5 23 36/21   HP 200 psi
15.5 knots

Complement
16 1st Cl.Passengers   nd Crew

SS RUTLAND

Dundee City Archives

SS RUTLAND was built for the Currie Line of Leith as Managers. Engines were installed at Dundee by Barclay Curle Ltd of Glasgow.
Lost in 1940 being sunk by U-124 South of Rockall after she had lost touch with convoy in heavy weather on passage Bermuda to Larne.[6]
The U-boat involved also sunk one cruiser, one corvette and 47 merchant ships before being sunk herself. The U-boat attacked on the surface after dark and one torpedo hit forward, the ship going down in 30 seconds.[1]

Built 1935   **Yard No** 349

Specifications
 1437 Gross tons
 260 x 40 x 26 feet

Machinery
Steam Triple Expansion by Barclay Curle
900 IHP
15 25 41/33   HP 200 psi
10 knots

Complement
0 Passengers   23 Crew

SS PHILOMEL

Dundee City Archives

SS Philomel was built for the General Steam Navigation Co. London for their Mediterranian Service from London.
In 1939 she was requisitioned before out break of War as a Transport and arrived in Alexandria August 1939 and served there .
In 1940 she was at the Falkland Islands to serve as an Ammunition Depot Ship for 1 year.
Drydocked in Cape Town and then served in south East Africa.
1945 Arrived Trincomalee.and served also Port Swettenham and Singapore. Returned to Owners.[6]

On fire at Lisbon 4/3/1947 after discharging cargo of motor cars but mail was destroyed for troops at Genoa and Naples.[1]
In 1957 sold to F.Iralo Groce A.P.A.Genoa for approx $100,000; renamed GROCE GUISSEPE Port of registry Genoa. Classed at Lloyds until July 1957.
In 1963 sold to Riakian Cia Nav S.A. [Clyptis & Scaivelis] Piraeus for £33,000; renamed ANESIS Port of Registry Piraeus.
1967 Aground 15 miles East of Lagos. On voyage from Doula to Spain and Beirut with logs; vessel broke in two and abandoned.[6]

Built 1935	**Yard No** 350

Specifications
 2115 Gross tons
 3000 x 45 x 28 feet
Machinery
Steam Triple Expansion by J G Kincaid
Greenock   1809 IHP
21 33 60/36   HP 220 psi
12.5 knots

Complement
12 Passengers   31 Crew

SS SHEKATIKA

SS SHEKATIKA was built for the Christian Salvesen Co.,Ltd., as Managers; for the Sydney, Cape Breton-Montreal coal trade. There are conflicting claims made for her sinking.

In 1940 she was Torpedoed and sunk by U-101 off Rockal, (U-123 has also been credited with this sinking), while on passage from Gaspe to Hartlepool. Survivors were landed at Greenock.[6]
Sunk by U99 (Commdr Otto Kretschmer the U Boat captain who sunk 350,000 tons before capture). U99 left Lorient on Oct 14 1940 and was back Oct 23 having sunk 9 ships and expended all torpedoes. After 4 days out on Oct 17-18 it attacked convoy SC7. Submarines U93, 100, 28, 123, 101, 99, 46 ordered to attack on Oct 17. U99 was too far away to join in the wolf pack attack but joined in the melee after the alarm was raised and moved in between the lines of the convoy in a bright hunter's moon. Torpedoes were fired from 700 yds but missed. A second torpedo hit another ship which sank in seconds. U99 also sank FISCUS*, THELIA, SEDGEPOOL and at a second attempt SKEKATIKA which was hit amidships and settled by the stern the crew abandoning ship. Kretschmer was welcomed on his return to Lorient by Admiral Doenitz. SHEKATIKA was homeward bound from Halifax with steel below and pit props piled high on deck but failed to keep up mainly because of poor quality Canadian bunker coal. She was ordered back to join a slower convoy coming up behind. Hit in No 4 hold with the tailshaft broken and the sea sluicing in to the engine room she was was abandoned in an orderly manner. She remained afloat because of the timber and two more torpedoes were required to sink her. [1] With reference therin to "The Golden Horseshoe" Kretschmer's biography by Terence Robertson.
*Robert Donald of Park Avenue Dundee, the writer's uncle, was the Second Engineer on FISCUS and died in this attack.[DM]

Built 1936	Yard No 351

Specifications
5458 Gross tons
406 x 55 x 30 feet

Machinery
Steam Triple Expansion by David Rowan
of Glasgow 1650 IHP (Rowans installed)
21.5 36 62/45   HP 225psi
10 knots

Complement
6 Passengers   35 Crew

SS BLACKHEATH

SS BLACKHEATH was built for Watts Watts & Co Ltd. She served as a supply ship during the Norwegian campaign in April-May 1940 during which she was berthed at a damaged quay at Namsos in the dark during a snowstorm without a pilot and against the advice of the captain of an accompanying destroyer. Discharge was possible only at night and the vessel put in four times under continuous bombing. The cargo of lorries ammunition and food were landed only for the ammo to be blown up while the ship was at sea. Towards the end of the campaign lorries and stores were loaded from Horsted and she was the last merchant ship to leave Norway. The Master was awarded the OBE in June 1940. Used as a supply ship in the Middle East she was torpedoed by U-870 and had her back broken near Gibraltar 10/1/45 inside the international zone off Tangier. The crew abandoned when the ship was struck but re-boarded in an attempt to save her without success but did manage to ground her to allow the cargo to be removed. Wreck abandoned and sold Oct 1945.

Built 1936   **Yard No** 353

Specifications
 4636 Gross tons
 410 x 56 x 37 feet

Machinery
Steam Triple expansion by NEM of
Wallsend 2000 IHP   23 38 65/42
HP 225 psi Superheated to 620F
10 knots

Complement
6 Passengers   38 Crew

TUG HARECRAIG

Steam tug and tender HARECRAIG was built for the Dundee Harbour Trust for a contract price of £22,256. In Dec 1938 she towed the Finnish barque ALASTOR in distress off GAA bank, Buddon Ness . Helped tow in CITY OF MARSEILLES mined off outer bouy Jan 1940. Scrapped at Inverkeithing (Thos. Ward) 1964.[1]

Built   1936   **Yard No** 354

Specifications
 202 Gross tons
  110 x 25 x 10 feet

Machinery
Steam Triple expansion (twin)
by Plenty of Newbury 600 SHP
10 16.5 27/18   HP 185 psi
11 knots

Complement
0 Passengers   7 Crew

MV MALLARD

MV MALLARD was built for The General Steam Navigation Co Ltd of London which was a regular customer of the Caledon yard.   Sister ship to MV PLOVER for which see separate entry.

Built   1936   **Yard No** 355

Specifications
351 Gross tons
  160 x 26 x 11 feet

Machinery
Diesel 500 BHP by British Auxiliaries
Glasgow (Atlas Diesel Stockholm) type
M44M 2 stroke single acting
4 Cyls 340mm x 570mm stroke
11 knots

Complement
0 Passengers   9 Crew

MV PLOVER

© The Courier D C Thomson & Co Ltd

MV PLOVER was built for the General Steam Navigation Co. Ltd. of London for the North French Ports Service.

Sister Ship to MALLARD and theirs was a double launch.

The above photograph shows the river scene after the double launch with a tug placing itself between the two hulls.[2] The debris in the water is the slip timbers from the launch.[DM]

Plover's engineroom was completely flooded at Boulogne in Dec 1950 because of a defective valve; beached and pumped out by the local fire brigade. She was floated , cargo discharged and towed to the Thames for repairs. In collision below Goole 5/9/54 with Dutch MV GAESTERLAND which was aground. Disabled with pump trouble after leaving Rotterdam for Gt.Yarmouth 28/5/59 and towed back to Rotterdam by MV LYNN TRADER. Sunk in collision with MV HOLLANDS DUIN, New Waterway 7/11/61 at Pernis. Pumped out and refloated with aid of sheerlegs and sold for scrap. [1]

1961 In Collision in New Waterway to Amsterdam and sank.

1961 Arrived at Jedrik Ido Ambacht for breaking up.[6]

Built 1936	Yard No 356

Specifications
 351 Gross tons
  160 x 26 x 11 feet

Machinery
Diesel 500 BHP by British Auxiliaries
Glasgow (Atlas Diesel Stockholm)
11 knots

Complement
0 Passengers   9 Crew

MV CHARON

MV CHARON was built for the Ocean S.S. Co., (Singapore-West Australian Ports Service) Alfred Holt & Co. managers. Fitted for cattle carrying. [2]

She left Freemantle 30/01/1942 but was turned back at Batavia (Djakarta) as Singapore was declared untenable. She was based at Sydney for the rest of the war and traded to New Guinea and the Pacific Isles and Numea. In peacetime CHARON and GORGON took up to 100,000 sheep a year to Singapore. After the war 20 milk cows were kept in each ship until the dairy industry recovered. Sold to Singapore scrappers in 1964 for £48,213 she re-emerged within a few weeks as SENG KONG No 1(Panama Flag). [1]

1965 sold to Liam Bee Co. and broken up at Singapore.[6]

At the time of the CHARON launch 15/10/36 Caledon had had 19 ships ordered in 18 months.[3]

Built 1936	**Yard No** 357

Specifications
 3703 Gross tons
 315 x 51 x 24 feet

Machinery
Diesel 6 cyl 2 stroke DA(double acting)
by B&W Copenhagen 3300BHP
450mm bore 1200mm stroke.
(Chain driven scavenging blower)
12.5 knots

Complement
118 Passengers 96 Crew

SS BACCHUS

© The Courier D C Thomson & Co

SS BACCHUS was built for the Admiralty Naval Stores Dept. as a water carrier and store ship and was able to distill its own cargo water. Prior to 1939 on the Malta run. Stationed mainly at Greenock and Scapa Flow. Became a distilling ship during WWII. Later she was a naval stores issuing ship in the Far East. Finally used on Fleet training duties UK-Malta-Far East. Steamed 1.3 million miles in commission.[1]
Sold in 1962 to Singapore Owners, Chip Hwo Shipping & Trading Company; Re -named PULAU BALI port of Registry, Panama.
1964 Broken up at Singapore; Surveys overdue and laid up at Singapore since November 1962. [6]

Built 1936   **Yard No** 358

Specifications
 3153 Gross tons
 320 x 49 x 25 feet

Machinery
Steam Triple expansion 2000 BHP
by NE Marine Newcastle.
21 35 58/42   HP 200psi
12 knots

Complement
44 officers and crew.

MV GLAMIS

MV GLAMIS was built for the D P & L Co. Ltd. Of Dundee. She grounded for 6.5 hours on the Abertay spit on the South side of the Tay in 1937 with slight damage.

Damaged in collision with MV BUENOS AIRES in the Thames on December 2nd 1938. Chartered for the Isle of Man service during WWII. On 16th May 1949 she was damaged in collision with the Panama registered SS SOCRATES in the Thames when the latter was going astern after colliding with GUERNSEY COAST. Windlass and other damage occurred to GLAMIS. She suffered main engine failure at 2.30 am on August 10 1957 3.5 miles South of Corton L/V while on voyage London to Dundee. She was towed to Great Yarmouth by tug Richard Lee Barker and sailed thereafter on August 12th.

Sold to Greek owners in 1964 and renamed REMYLIA classed 100A1 at Lloyds for Black Sea and Red Sea service. REMYLIA damaged in collision with SS ANGELIKI in Pireus harbour 20/08/1963. Sold at Pireus in 1964 and renamed AGIOS SPYRIDONES and subsequently had various names and owners subsequently being the ROLA in 1980 of the Union Progress Co. of Limassol.

In 1979 she was on the Limassol to Alexandria run with 900 tons of cement in bags when water entered the engine room via the sterntube. The pumps could not cope and she was beached near Brules L/H on January 12th. She was floated off with portable pumps on board on 17/1/1980 and towed towards Alexandria by two Egyptian Navy tugs.[1]

Built   1936   **Yard No** 359

Specifications
555 Gross tons
165 x 30 x 14 feet

Machinery
Diesel 500 BHP 4 cyl 2 stroke SA diesel
by British Auxiliaries Glasgow (Polar
Atlas Diesel Stockholm)
4cyl 340 bore 570 stroke
11 knots

Complement
0 Passengers   11 Crew

MV GOLDFINCH

MV GOLDFINCH (sister ship BULLFINCH) was built for the General Steam Navigation Co. Ltd of London. She evacuated 1500 troops from Dunkirk in May 1940 arriving off La Penne beaches at 4.50 am on 29th May. Beaches were crowded with troops with few boats to remove them. The troops were ordered back to the beach. Lines were put ashore and boats hauled back and forth under continous bomber attacks all day. The ship floated at 6.15 am while air attacks continued. Troops fixed two Bren guns and manned the ship's Lewis gun. Two planes were shot down. The troops were disembarked at Ramsgate while Spitfires beat off German planes. A plaque bearing the arms of Dunkirk was presented to the ship in 1949. She was sold to British flag owners in 1949.[1]

1962 To Allen Shipping Line Ltd.; Re named ALLEN COMMODORE Port of Registry Guernsey. Sold in 1966 To Helene T. Vavatsioules,Thesaloniki [Salonica] for £23,600; renamed THEODORUS. Port of Registry Thesaloniki.

Sold in 1969 To P.Dalgas.G.Konidaris and N.Soukes,Thesaloniki; renamed SAMATA Port of Registry Thesaloniki. In 1973 Reverted back to THEODORUS.

1976 sold to Meganissi Shipping Co.,Ltd., [G. Konidaris & P. Palmos]; renamed SAMATA II Port of Registry Piraeus.

1984 Broken up at Eleusis, Greece.[6]

Built 1936	**Yard No** 361

Specifications
453 Gross tons
170 x 31 x 11 feet

Machinery
Diesel 420 BHP by British Auxiliaries
Glasgow.(Polar Atlas) 6cyl @ 250mm
420mm stroke
10.25 knots

Complement
0 Passengers   16 Crew

SS BUNGAREE

Slinging a boiler

Lifting aboard

SS BUNGAREE (sister ship to BELTANA, see next page) was built for the Adelaide Steamship Company of Adelaide Australia. Shown approaching the Boilershop after launch.[2]

1940 Requisitioned by R.A.N. Became H.M.A.S. BUNGAREE Minelayer [423 Mines].

1947 Resumed Commercial Service.

1957 sold to Kowloon Navigation Co., Ltd.; Renamed DAMPIER ; H.C. Sleigh,Ltd., Managers Hong Kong.

1960 sold to Pan Norse S.S. Co., S.A.,; Renamed EASTERN MARINER Port of Registry Panama.

1963 sold to Mariner Ocean Transport Co., S.A., Panama.

Mined 8m. below Saigon, shelled and sank in shallow water Constructive Total Loss. Later Salvaged by Japanese; Renamed KITIGAWA MARU No 15. Towed to Hong Kong.

In 1968 under Demolition by Kwan Ho, Hong Kong.[6]

Built 1937 **Yard No** 362

Specifications
453 Gross tons
350 x 48 x 33 feet

Machinery
Steam triple expansion by J G Kincaid of Greenock.
20.5 33 54/42   HP 220psi
11.3 knots

Complement
0 Passengers   16 Crew

SS BELTANA

Dundee City Archives

SS BELTANA (sister ship to BUNGAREE) was built for the Adelaide Steamship Company of Adelaide Australia. She went aground entering Adelaide on 14/12/1949.
Grounded Port Philip bay 19/4/1952 when on voyage from Melbourne to Freemantle.
She struck a reef at Port Philip in 1963. Beached 30 miles from Melbourne on the Mornington Peninsula* with a cargo of 4000 tons of steel and 400 tons of general cargo and sustained extensive bottom damage. Sold in damaged condition and towed Hong Kong and scrapped in 1964.[1]

*1963 Stranded and became constructive loss; Struck Corsair Rock in Rip Channel at Port Philip Heads; Beached on Mornington Peninsula.
Sold to William Charlick Ltd. in damaged condition, towed to Hong Kong and Broken up.[6]

Built   1937   **Yard No** 363

Specifications
 453 Gross tons
 350 x 48 x 33 feet

Machinery
Steam triple expansion by J G Kincaid of Greenock.
20.5 33 54/42   HP 220psi
11.3 knots

Complement
0 Passengers   16 Crew

SS ABOYNE

Dundee City Archives

SS ABOYNE was built for the Aberdeen Newcastle and Hull steamship company of Aberdeen, R.C.Cowper Managers.

She was a convoy rescue ship Oct. 1943 to June 1945 assisting 26 convoys and picking up 20 survivors. She used her forward derrick for transfer of doctors and patients to and from other ships of the convoy. 60 cases were transferred without a hitch. The plan was evolved by chief officer Hughes who had experience of discharging by derrick into surf boats on the West African coast. Her rudder was damaged while assisting USA freighter THEODORE PARKER in a heavy gale and she was taken in tow by the frigate DEVERON. She rescued three airmen from the "Mac*" ships EMPIRE McCOLL and GADILA (Dutch). She returned to the DP&L Co after the war and was sold to the Clyde Shipping Co after 3 months of charter and renamed ARKLOW. In 1947 she was sold to the Ulster Steamship Co. Ltd. Belfast, G. Heyn, Managers for £85,000; renamed FAIR HEAD Port of Registry Belfast. She saved the Dutch crew of MV PETO mined and sunk 10 miles North of Terschelling Bank L.V. 22/8/52.

1958 sold to Hellenic Mediteranian Lines Co. Ltd. Greece; renamed LIGURIA; Port of Registry Piraeus.[1]

1960 sold to Athanassiades Greece; renamed THOMAS H; port of Registry Piraeus.

In 1963 caught fire South of Sicily : Pos'n 36' 45'N., 14'35'E; Beached near Scalambri. Burnt out and abandoned; CTL on passage Clatz Romnia to Liverpool with timber.[6]

* Merchant aircraft carriers

Built 1936   **Yard No** 364

Specifications
 1020 Gross tons
 350 x 48 x 33 feet

Machinery
Steam triple expansion 1800 IHP by J G Kincaid of Greenock.
19 32.5 56/42   HP 220psi
13.2 knots

Complement
0 Passengers   24 Crew

SS NORMAN MONARCH

Dundee City Archives

SS NORMAN MONARCH was built for the Monarch steamship company of Glasgow, Raeburn & Verel Managers.
1941 Sunk by U-Boat [Possibly U-94] S.E. of Cape Farewell Greenland, whilst in Convoy HX126 from Halifax, Newfoundland, to U.K. with full cargo of wheat.[6]
Torpedoed 20/5/1941 and crew of 40 and 8 gunners taken off by HARPAGUS; 26 lost when HARPAGUS was sunk later the same day.
A replacement NORMAN MONARCH was built at the Caledon yard in 1942. [1]

Built 1937   **Yard No** 365

Specifications
 4718 Gross tons
 425 x 26 x 27 feet

Machinery
Steam triple expansion 2100 IHP by J G
Kincaid of Greenock.
23.5 39.5 66/45   HP 220 psi
11.5 knots

Complement
0 Passengers   44 Crew

MV HERON

Heron workers at launch

MV HERON was built for the General Steam navigation Co. Ltd. Of London.
For their Mediterranean service.
1939 Requisitioned before start of War as transport. Based in Scottish waters.
1942 Moved to Australian waters & Used as depot ship. Latterly with the Pacific fleet.
Arrived Singapore and returned to owners.
1956 sold to Moss Hutchinson Line Liverpool; Renamed KUFRA.
1979 broken up by Brodospas at Split,Yugoslavia. [6]
Evacuated Fleet Air Arm personnel from Harsted Norway June 1940. Refitted on the Clyde and sent out to Alexandria via the Cape in a convoy which lost several ships. On arrival examination of the bottom revealed scores caused by a U-boat which dived below her.
Imprisoned in the Suez Canal when the Germans mined both ends. After release she worked in the Red Sea and East Africa transferring ammo to small carriers for the fleet. Some crew were wounded in Japanese raids on Colombo. 14 months depot ship at Aden. Grounded in fog off Monklands Wharf at Glasgow 24/10/1957 on voyage from Glasgow to Iskerendun. Her bow struck the North side of Barclay Curle's shipyard.
Arab league blacklisted KUFRA for carrying strategic materials to Israel and was not allowed to enter Arab ports.[1]

Built 1937	**Yard No** 366

Specifications
 2373 Gross tons
 300 x 45 x 28 feet

Machinery
Diesel 2200 BHP. Engine manufactured by
Sulzer of Winterthur Switzerland.
4 cyl 600mm stroke 1040mm
12.5 knots
Complement
12 Passengers   nd Crew

SS BECKENHAM

SS BECKENHAM was built for Watts Watts & Co. Ltd. Of London. On 24/3/43 she was damaged by a mine explosion near Tripoli. In 1945 she survived heavy storm damage en route from Montreal to Halifax NS. She survived severe grounding on the coast of Brazil at Tutula Bar in 1946 and was refloated but lost her rudder and sternframe and sprung the aft peak bulkhead. She was towed to the Tyne for repairs.

She survived grounding at Schelde in 1947 and was in collision with MV METHAN in 1948. Chartered by P&O in 1950 to load at Southampton for Australia 500 cars in crates and another 50 in parts for assembly.[1]

In 1953 she was wrecked near Cape Ratmanova, Kara Sea, North Russia on passage from Igarka to London. Later she broke her back and became total loss. The vessel was on time charter to Russians. Navigation of the ship had been taken over entirely by Russian Officers. All Watts Watts Officers Exonerated without need for M.O.T. enquiry; crew taken to Archangel.[6]

Engines and boilers were made and installed by NEM at Wallsend. The ship was towed to the Tyne and returned to Dundee under her own power.[3]

Built 1937	**Yard No** 367

Specifications
 4636 Gross tons
 410 x 56 x 28 feet

Machinery
Steam triple expansion 1600 IHP by NEM
of Wallsend 23 38 65/42   HP 220 psi
11 knots

Complement
nd Passengers   nd Crew

TSMV GLENEARN

Dundee City Archives

TSMV GLENEARN was built for the Glen Line.
1939 Taken over by Admiralty and converted to a Fast Fleet Supply Ship.
1940 Further conversion into Infantry Assault Ship.
1946 Released to Owners. 1947 Returned to Far East Route. In 1950 Attacked by a Chinese Nationalist Plane in Formosa Strait and slightly damaged; two crew members injured.
1970 Arrived at Kaochsiung Taiwan for Demolition; Chinese Nationalist Government paid £11,600 compensation for above incident in 1950.[6]
There was a steel shortage in late 1937 during the time this ship was building.[3]

pto

Built 1938   **Yard No** 368

Specifications
8986 Gross tons
475 x 66 x 38 feet

Machinery
Diesel 12000 BHP twin screw by Burmeister and Wain of Copenhagen. 6cyl 620mm dia 1400 stroke 2 stroke direct reversible
18 knots

Complement
12 Passengers 83 Crew

HMS GLENEARN

(continued)

HMS GLENEARN was assigned in a group in November 1940 along with GLENGYLE and GLENROY to Operation Workshop an object of this being the capture of Pantellaria, an Italian island between Sicily and Tunisia, deploying 3500 commando troops carried by the group. There was no harbour and landing craft were to be used. The project was postponed until January 1941 and then abandoned. The three ships switched to the Dodecanese project and were on hand for the evacuation of Greece i.e. operation Demon. These were the first of 8 ships of a new class. Commissioned in 1940 as a naval auxiliary LSI- 1087 troops and sent to Nauplia (Morea) Greece 24/4/1941 during the evacuation of Greece. Accompanied by cruiser PHOEBE, destroyers STUART and VOYAGER, corvette HYACINTH and transport ULSTER PRINCE, GLENEARN was dive bombed resulting in minor damage with fire. She steamed stern to wind until the fire was extinguished.

ULSTER PRINCE grounded in the fairway and was abandoned and was bombed by Germans the following day . GLENEARN carried the lighters which ferried the troops from shore. 6,685 men were taken off during the night of April 24/5 and GLENEARN returned to Crete without anchors. She returned to Nauplia during the night of April 26-27th/4/41 accompanied by the cruiser CALCUTTA destroyers ISIS, HOTSPUR, GRIFFIN and DIAMOND and troopers SLEMAT and KHEDIVE ISMAIL. GLENEARN was hit in the engineroom which was flooded and she was towed back to Crete by GRIFFIN. Loss of GLENEARN lighters severly handicapped the evacuation. The attack which was by JU88s began just before dark. GLENEARN lighters were put ashore at Menemusasia and used during later evacuation. Cruiser PERTH and destroyer STUART were sent to replace GLENEARN but several thousand men were left behind. Air attacks continued. GLENEARN was towed to Suda-bay Alexandria by the sloop GRIMSBY.

GLENEARN was one of the first ships to land troops in Normandy on D Day 6/6/44. She was in refugee service in the Far East Sept–Oct 1945 along with hospital ship GERUSALEMME . Evacuated 700 POWs from Hainer Island to Hong Kong.

Attacked by Chinese Nationalist aircraft in Formosa channel 15/7/50 when bound from Hamburg and London to Tsingtao and Yokohama. Bridge and steering gear damaged and crew injured requiring ship to put into Nagasaki. Chinese Government paid £11,638 damages in 1954.

Discharged last cargo December 1970 and was then sold for demolition at Kaochsiang. [1]

MV SEAFORTH

MV SEAFORTH was built for the Elder Dempster Co.
Torpedoed in the North Atlantic 18/2/41, under command of Captain W. Minns, 350 miles West of Lewis.
Total complement of 10 passengers and 49 crew lost.[1]

Built 1938   **Yard No** 369

Specifications
4199 Gross tons
370 x 52 x 25 feet

Machinery
Diesel 3540 BHP by Doxford of
Sunderland. 4 Cyls 560 mm 2160mm
stroke
12.5 knots

Complement
12 Passengers   58 Crew

SS BAROSSA

SS BAROSSA was built for the Adelaide Steamship Co. of Adelaide, Australia.

There was a westerly gale at the launch driving her down to West Ferry and three tugs were needed to get her to the Boilershop. Tug HARECRAIG was called in urgently. Damaged by Japanese aircraft at Port Darwin 19/2/42.[1]

Completed trial runs on Burntisland measured mile and handed over.

1964 delivered at Sydney to Cambay Prince S.S. Co., Ltd.; Registered in Hong Kong to Cronulla Shipping Price £50,000.

Renamed CRONULLA Port of Registry Panama.

1965 Transferred to San Jeronimo S.S. Co., Panama; John Manners & Co., Ltd., Managers, name unchanged.

1967 To Jaguar Shipping Corp., Ltd. Hon Kong. Panamanian Flag.

1969 Grounded entering Hong Kong on Wen Leng Island, refloated with substantial damage.

1969 delivered for demolition by Moller & Co. at Hong Kong.[6]

.

Built 1938	**Yard No** 370

Specifications
 4238 Gross tons
 360 x 50 x 27 feet

Machinery
Steam Triple Expansion 1825 SHP by J G Kincaid of Greenock
20.5 33 54/42   HP 220 psi
11 knots

Complement
0 Passengers   43 Crew

SS KOORINGA

SS KOORINGA was built for M'Ilwraith M'Eacharn Ltd., Melbourne; Port of Registry Melbourne; Trials at Burntisland.
Damaged in a multi collision in Freemantle in June 1946. In 1959 broke moorings in a gale at Kartasu on the West coast of Japan.[1]
1958 To Cambay Prince S.S.; Renamed STRAITS BREEZE Port of Registry Hong Kong; Manners, Hong Kong Managers.
1965 To San Fernardo S.S. Co., Panama; Renamed SAN EDUARDO Port of register Panama; John Manners as Managers.
1965 To Teh Foo Nav.,Co.,Ltd., Kaohsuing Taiwan.
1966 Renamed TEH FOO Laid up.
1968 Arrived at Kaohsuing for breaking up.[6]

Built 1937	Yard No 371

Specifications
3291 Gross tons
360 x 49 x 32 feet

Machinery
Steam triple expansion 1825 IHP (with Bauer Wach exh turbine) manufactured by Barclay Curle Glasgow.
20 32 52/42   HP 220 psi
11 knots

Complement
0 Passengers   45 Crew

TSMV GLENGYLE

Dundee City Archives

TSMV GLENGYLE was built for the Glen Line of Liverpool, part of the Alfred Holt group.
1939 Taken over by the Admiralty.and converted to fast Fleet supply Ship.
1940 Further conversion to Landing Ship Infantry LS[l]
1946 returned to Owners (see opposite for war service record).
1948 Rebuilt and delivered to Glen Line
1970 Transferred to Blue Funnel's Ocean S.S. Co.; Renamed DEUCALION .
1971 Arriving at Kaohsiung,Taiwan for breaking up.[6]

See opposite.

See opposite.

Built 1939	**Yard No** 372

Specifications
 9919 Gross tons
 475 x 66 x 38 feet

Machinery
Diesel 12000 BHP by B&W Copenhagen
6Cyls 620mm   stroke 1400mm
18 knots

Complement
12 Passengers   83 Crew

HMS GLENGYLE

(continued)

The fifth of that name, was built in 1939 by Caledon SB & E Co, Dundee, as one of the Glenearn Class of fast motor vessels ordered for the Glen Line, part of the Alfred Holt Group, Liverpool, to operate a twice-monthly service on the Far East routes. On delivery she was taken over by the Admiralty and converted into a fast supply ship, flying the white ensign as HMS GLENGYLE. Subsequently, from April 1940 a conversion was undertaken to make her an unarmoured Landing Ship Infantry (L) capable of carrying 700 troops. She retained a conveyor and two lifting derricks, one forward one aft to be used to lift out MLC's (Motorised Landing Craft). Space was provided for 12 LCA's (Landing Craft Assault) and 1 SLC (Support Landing Craft), with 12 special heavy duty davits to carry the LCA's which could be used as lifeboats if the ship was in danger of sinking. The LSI(L) were heavily armed for that time with eight twin 2 pdr Pompoms, four 2 pdr guns and eight 20 mm Oerlikons.

After contributing to the training of the first commandos at Inveraray she had a lively wartime career: participating in the evacuation of Greece, the Battle for Crete, the Malta convoys, commando raids on Bardia, Litani River and Dieppe, invasion landings at Oran, Sicily and Salerno. Then, after a major refit was off to the Far East to carry troops to the relief of Hong Kong and Singapore, RAAF personnel to join the occupation forces in Japan and, finally, to bring freed POWs home to the Clyde.

When the ship was returned to Glen Line on 17th July 1946 priority in the overcrowded and overstretched shipyards was being given to the refurbishment of food ships. Consequently, refurbishment was slow and it was not until 3rd March 1948 that MV GLENGYLE rejoined the fleet after being refitted for commercial operations by Vickers Armstrong at Newcastle. In October 1970 she was transferred to Blue Funnel and renamed DEUCALION but only until June of the following year when she was broken up at Kaohsiung. [3]

Similar assignment to GLENEARN. Converted to a commando assault ship at John Brown's yard Clydebank. Battle honours inscribed on a wooden scroll on the ship were Bardia, Raphtis, Raphina, Sphakia, Litani River, Dieppe, Oran, Pachino, Salerno, Anzio. She took part in 10 major operations steaming 125,000 miles.

Converted as an auxiliary to carry fuel and ammo in support of force to hunt German battleship Graf Spee. Converted to a troop ship to carry 697 commando troops.

Arrived in the Med in January 1941 and supported a raid on Bardia , a main enemy supply depot. In the evacuation of Greece April 1941 she took off 5700 men in the dark from Raphtis a small port south of Athens and sailed at 4am for Suda Bay Crete.

With a Naval escort she took off 8200 men from Raphina. In operation Demon i.e. the evacuation of Greece she took off 50,672 troops. After taking 700 Argyle and Sutherland Highlanders to Crete a battle ensued requiring the evacuation of Crete.

Embarked 8000 troops from Naval escorts at Sphakia on 29/5/41 and took them to Alexandria in one lift. Involved in the Syrian campaign in 1941 then training British and ANZAC troops in the Bitter lakes, Suez canal.

Jan 5-8 1942 sailed Alexandria to Malta with munitions, milk, food, coke and coal and was the first arrival for several weeks. Straddled by bombs in Malta dry dock.

Returned to UK early 1942 and was one of six ships sent to Oran North Africa on a commando raid and also to land US troops. After Sicily landings she was sent to the Far East via Bombay. Returned to the Med for the Italy operations in which she survived heavy bombing raids at Salerno and Anzio. Sent to the Far East and took the 3rd Commando Brigade to occupy Hong Kong. Carried out refugee service in the Far East and was on loan to the Australian Government carrying a large force to open up Singapore. In January 1946 transported 900 Australian troops to Japan. Decommissioned after 5yrs and 10 months service and returned to the Glen Line Far East service after conversion by Vickers Armstrong at Walker on Tyne. In 1970 transferred to the Blue Funnel Line and renamed DUECADON. Sold to a Formosan company in 1971. [1]

TSMV GLENARTNEY

TSMV GLENARTNEY was built for the Glen line of Glasgow and like TSMV GLENGYLE was commandeered for war service by the UK Government. The Glen Line was part of the Alfred Holt Group.
It is known from Caledon records that TSMV GLENARTNEY had conversion for war service done at Dundee.
Ref: Ship technical notebooks GD324/5/4/8.[2]
Rescued part of the crew of liner CAMARIA destroyed by fire in the North Atlantic in April 1941.
On refugee service in the Far East Sept/Oct 1945. Sold to Japanese scrappers in 1971.[1]

Short funnel, Stump Masts and Polemast offset on port side of Bridge.
1941 Taken over by Admiralty as Fast Supply Ship.
1946 Released to Owners for conversion back to cargo service. 1947 Returned to theFar East run.
1967 Sold for £140,000. Left Kobe for Onomichi; April demolition commenced.[6]

.

Built 1939   **Yard No** 373

Specifications
8986 Gross tons
475 x 66 x 38 feet

Machinery
Diesel 12000 BHP by B&W Copenhagen
6Cyls 620mm stroke 1400mm
18 knots

Complement
12 Passengers 83 Crew

SS BUNDALEER

Dundee City Archives

SS BUNDALEER was built for the Adelaide Steamship company. Her trial trip took place off Burntisland in March 1939 in a heavy gale with the pilot cutter sheltering on return. Trials party spent most of the night at sea. Sold to Pacific Navigation Co 1960 renamed FUCHING. Dragged both anchors in Typhoon Ruby in Sept 1964 and ran aground. Refloated and no leakage found. In 1964 she was transferred to the Ocean Trader Navigation Company of Panama and renamed ORIENTAL TRADER.

She was renamed DORINTHIA in 1966 under new ownership of the Panamanian Oriental Steamship Co. Finally renamed ARENA when bought by the Great Taipei Navigation company and in 1969 was sold to Kaohsiung scrappers.[1] [6]

Built   1939   **Yard No** 374

Specifications
 4237 Gross tons
 360 x 50 x 28 feet

Machinery
Steam triple expansion by G J Kincaid of Greenock   1265IHP
20.5 33 54/42   HP 220psi
12 knots

Complement
0 Passengers   43 Crew

TSSS SCOTT

Twin screw Survey Sloop SCOTT was built for the British Admiralty and was basically a Halcyon class minesweeper.
She was originally completed as a Survey vessel and was converted for Minesweeping during 1939-45 War at the end of which she reverted back to being a Survey Vessel. 1965 Broken up. [6]

Built as a surveying sloop by the British Admiralty she was launched by Lady Skelton wife of Engineer Vice Admiral Sir Roy Skelton who superintended the building of DISCOVERY in 1901 and was Chief Engineer of that ship in the Antarctic. Her first survey after completion was in the Tay 1939. Battle Honours of SCOTT included Norway 1941, Normandy June 6- July 3 1944. She took part in the Lofotens Raid in 22-28 December 1941. In 1951 he was used in the Channel search for the missing submarine HMS AFFRAY. In 1960 she located 23 wrecks in the Channel all above the 40 feet safety level required for supertankers. One of these the SEA SERPENT, sunk in 1916, was located at 33 feet deep. Decommisioned 1965 by MoD (Navy Dept) and sent to W H Arnott Young's West of Scotland breakers yard.[1]
In the search of the BISMARCK she was sent out ahead of HMS HOOD and HMS PRINCE of WALES to establish the position of the edge of the ice off Greenland.[Halcyon Class home page – web].

Built   1938   **Yard No** 375

Specifications
1013 Gross tons
230 x 33 x 23 feet

Machinery
Steam Turbine compound 2x1770 SHP
twin screw.
17 knots

Complement   80 Crew (as minesweeper)

SS TAMBUA

SS TAMBUA was built for the Colonial Sugar Refining Company of Sydney NSW as a molasses and general cargo carrier. Molasses was carried in cantilever tanks and dry cargo in the holds. She presented a design problem because of the distance of her intended voyages from Sydney to Fiji.[2]

Grounded at Towsville, Australia in 1963 and 1967 [1]

Ran trials from Tees Fairway to Saltscar Rock.

1969 Sold to Pae Treacle Nav., Co., Panamanian; Renamed MARIA ROSA. Port of Registry Panama; Owners actually Taiwanese.

1973 Broken up at Kaohsiung, Taiwan, by Chin Ho Fa Iron & Steel Co.[6]

Built 1938   **Yard No** 376

Specifications
3565 Gross tons
360 x 50 x 24feet

Machinery
Steam triple expansion 1450IHP by NEM Wallsend
21.5 36 62/42   HP 220psi
10.5 knots

Complement
0 Passengers   41 Crew

SS BEACONSFIELD

SS BEACONSFIELD was built for the Watts Watts shipping company of London.
On fire in dry dock at Shields August 20 1947 when a hole had to be cut in its side to get at the fire. She was the last Watts Watts pre-war ship in service when sold to Hong Kong owners for £94,500 in October 1958 and renamed TWINHORSE. Later owned by Queensland Shipping Co renamed NASSAU. She had been laid up at Fowey for 5 months when sold to Japanese scrappers at £14 per ton light displacement.[1]

1938 Ran trials off River Tyne, in loaded condition.
1958 Sold for £94,500 to Malay Shipping Co., Ltd., British Pacific Export & Import Co., Ltd., Managers
1964 Broken up in Japan after lying in China with bottom damage.[6]

Built 1938	**Yard No** 377

Specifications
 4634 Gross tons
 410 x 56 x 28 feet

Machinery
Steam 1600 IHP by NEM of Wallsend
23 23 38/42   HP 220 psi
11 knots

Complement
 0 Passengers   39 Crew

SS SCOTTISH MONARCH

Dundee City Archives

SS SCOTTISH MONARCH was built for the Monarch Steamship Company of Glasgow. Raeburn and Verel, Managers.
She cost £139,292 when new. A replacement was built at the Caledon in 1943.[1]

Ran trials from Tay Fairway to North Carr Light Vessel.
In 1941 when bound U.K. to Freetown she was sunk by U-105 South of Cape Verde Islands.[6]

Built   1938   **Yard No** 378

Specifications
 4719 Gross tons
 425 x 56 x 27 feet

Machinery
Steam Triple expansion 2100 IHP by
J G Kincaid of Greenock HP 220psi
23.5 39.5 66/45
12 knots

Complement
 0 Passengers   44 Crew

Lightship ABERTAY

© The Courier D C Thomson & Co Ltd

Lightship ABERTAY was built for the Dundee Harbour Trust at a cost of £36,000.
Towed to Gap A by PHAROS's Capt David Mearns in charge. Gap A was the West end of a gap in a 35 mile deep minefield off the coast of Angus. A 3 month duty was the normal posting. She was withdrawn early in the 1939-45 war and anchored off Woodhaven.
After VE day in 1945 she was moored 45 miles off Montrose to mark Gap A in a defensive minefield. On May 13th 1945 she was hailed by a U-Boat which wanted to surrender. She became an automated light float in 1971 monitored from Dundee harbour. Hull with colour changed from red to black. This was the first automatic light float in Europe.[1]

1971 modified, automatic classed: Light Float Unmanned. Conversion cost £120,000.
1984 withdrawn from station and laid up.
1985 To The Corporation of Trinity House as spare L/V; served as test rig for Trinity House Automation programe at Harwich.
1992 Broken up.[6]

Built   1939   **Yard No** 379

Specifications
 267 Gross tons
 104 x 26 x 14 feet

Machinery
No propulsion. Generators (3) by Davey
Paxman of Colchester

Complement
0 Passenger   6 Crew

SS BARWEN

SS BARWEN was built for the Hoddart Parker shipping Company of Melbourne Australia.
In collision Newcastle NSW 21/6/1946. On fire en route Melbourne- Freemantle 1965. Reported disabled en route Geraldton-Bell Bay with manganese ore but able to maintain steerage way. Engine compounded and arrived Adelaide 21/6/65.
1972 She dragged anchors and stranded with her engine room flooded at Kaiohsiung from Saigon with a tug and four tractors on deck. Abandoned as constructive total loss.[1]
Trials on Burtisland Measured Mile; Converted to Oil Fuel.
1961 To McIlwraith McEacharn; Port of Registry Melbourne.
1964 To Associated Steamships P/L.
1969 To Wing Cn S.S. Co., S.A., Panamanian; Renamed ABILITY Port of Registry, Panama.
Renamed NEW ABILITY; Port of Registry Singapore; same Owners.
1972 Ashore at Kaohsiung, Taiwan; Later declared Constructive Total Loss.[6]

Built 1939	**Yard No** 380

Specifications
 4238 Gross tons
 360 x 50 x 27 feet

Machinery
Steam triple expansion 1825 IHP by J G Kincaid of Greenock
20.5 33 54/42   HP 220 psi
12 knots

Complement
 0 Passengers   43 Crew

TSMV HESPERUS

© The Courier D C Thomson & Co Ltd

TSMV HESPERUS was built for the Northern Lighthouse Board.
Based at Oban replacing a vessel of the same name built by Gourlays of Dundee in 1896. During a gale in 1950 she towed the puffer CORPACH in distress off Kerrera with engine trouble. Withdrawn from the Oban station in 1963 for a £75,000 modernisation programme at Ardrossan Dockyard prior to transfer to Granton. New bridge and wheelhouse full width of the ship. At Granton summer 1964 (renamed POLE STAR) and sold for scrap.[1]

Built 1939   **Yard No** 381

Specifications
 843 Gross tons
 200 x 35 x 15 feet

Machinery
Twin Diesel 1300 BHP collective by
British Auxiliaries (Polar) of Glasgow.
4cyl 340 bore 570 stroke
 13.8 knots

Complement
 4 Passengers   37 Crew

MV ATHELVICTOR

MV ATHELVICTOR was built for the ATHEL Line of Liverpool.(Original name SILENUS)

Built as SILENUS for Swedish owners and sold to the Athel line after trials for about £300,000. Arrived Lagos from Tokoradi 4/12/1942. Following morning began discharge of benzene 60 tons of which leaked into the sea due to valve being left open. The benzene took fire on the sea and burnt three trawlers. Depth charges in the trawlers blew up and all three sank. The blast extinguished the fire which had killed 68 people. The Nigerian Govt. claimed damages of £136,000 and the Admiralty was awarded £117,000 in 1945. She suffered a broken crankshaft 200 miles from Thursday Island 12/12/46 on voyage from Abadan to Wellington. The Poop was damaged in collision with SS ESSO CARDIFF at Eastham 1/6/1950.[1]

Launched as SILENUS . Strengthened for Navigation in ice.

Only provisional trials carried out on River Tay due to Wartime conditions.

1940 Sold to Athel Lines Ltd. For about £300,000 after trials; Renamed ATHEL VICTOR.

1952 Sold to Chiarella Societe di Navigation, Genoa for £735,000; Re-Named CALIFORNIA; Port of Registry Genoa. 1960 Sold to Garla Cameli, Genoa for £132,000.

1961 To Armatorati Mediterraea Idorabutt, Palermo.

1962 sold to Italian Breakers at La Spezia.[6]

Built 1940	**Yard No** 382
Specifications 8320 Gross tons 458 x 59 x 35 feet	
Machinery Diesel 4300 BHP 4 stroke SA by Hawthorn Leslie of Newcastle (Gotaverken type) Cyls 8x650mm dia 1400mm stroke 12.5 knots	
Complement 1 Passengers 40 Crew	

MV MORIALTA

MV MORIALTA was built for the Adelaide Steamship Company.

When the order was received Caledon were told that the only dimensions that mattered were length and draft.[2]

One of the last vessels to get engines from Burmeister and Wain before the Germans occupied Copenhagen. She was commandeered before completion and fitted out as a troop carrier. Worked as a leave ship at Scrabster. Survived bomb attack in 1940. In May 1941, after the Lofotens raid, she brought 215 prisoners and 10 Quislings back to Scrabster. Figured in the film of the raid. King George VI reviewed the fleet from her bridge at Scapa flow. In 1944 she was transferred to the Med and was mined off Menton, France Sept 21 1944 but reached port. She did not reach Australia until 1946 and was used in the St Vincent Gulf service. Renamed WAIKEN by new owners John Burke Ltd she carried 53 passengers on the Queensland coast trade from Brisbane to Thursday Island. Sold to New Hebrides owners in 1964 and renamed JÁQUARDEL for service among the South Pacific islands. Her last owners named her ISLAND PEARL and in the Mekong Delta she capsized en route from Phnom Penh to Singapore with a cargo of rubber and cartridge scrap. Her crew was saved leaving the wreck lying in 25 feet of water clear of the channel where she was declared a total loss.[1]

Requisitioned by M.O.W.T. for Troop Service.

1940 War Service. On Pentland Ferry service Scrabster to Stromness. [North of Scotland, Orkney and Shetland Steam Navigation Co.,Ltd., Aberdeen as Acting Managers] [6]

Built   1940   **Yard No** 383

Specifications
1378 Gross tons
215 x 39 x 16 feet

Machinery
Diesel 2035 BHP by Burmeister and Wain
Copenhagen 2 stroke SA
Cyls 5x 500 Dia 900mm stroke
12.5 knots

Complement
16 Passengers   29 Crew

SS TOTTENHAM

SS TOTTENHAM was built for the Watts Watts shipping company.
Sister ships SS TWICKENHAM and SS TEDDINGTON were also built by the Caledon at this time.
She was en route from the Tyne to a French Atlantic port with coal on her maiden voyage when France capitulated and she was ordered to the USA where the cargo was discharged at Seattle. The surface raider ATLANTIS sunk her on 17/6/41 300 miles NW of Ascension Is where some crew were lost and the others taken to Germany as prisoners. Later 17 crew were picked up by MAHRONDE JURE.[1]

Price was originally £131,300.
1941 Sunk by German Commerce Raider ATLANTIS in South Atlantic. Bound Alexandria from U.K.[6]

Built 1940	**Yard No** 384

Specifications
 4761 Gross tons
 410 x 56 x 37 feet

Machinery
Steam triple expansion 2000 IHP by NEM of Newcastle
23 38 65/42   HP 220psi
10 knots

Complement
 0 Passengers   44 Crew inc gunners

SS TWICKENHAM and SS TEDDINGTON
(Identical to SS TOTTENHAM)

SS TWICKENHAM was torpedoed off the Canary Islands 15/7/43 on passage from Methil to River Plate with coal. The torpedo had hit the starboard bow and she was abandoned an hour later down by the head and with reports of bulkheads giving way. Corvette HMS GERANIUM picked up the crew and stood by on orders of the senior officer of the convoy. Master Capt. W D Wilson with 5 volunteers reboarded TWICKENHAM the following morning, steam was raised and course set for Dakar 950 miles away.

It was judged too dangerous to go ahead and ship would not steer astern. Drifting South GERANIUM tried three times to attach a towline, the propeller being fouled by the line but cleared by the boarding party. Tug SHELDT attached a line and towed TWICKENHAM stern first for 200 miles but developed boiler trouble and had to depart. Weather fined away and TWICKENHAM steamed forward at 4 knots with damaged bows. She reached Dakar on 31/7/43. Capt. Wilson and Chief Engineer were awarded the OBE. 18 months later TWICKENHAM sailed home to the Tyne with false bows and the Caledon supplied frames for the new bow.

In Oct 1946 TWICKENHAM inaugurated the Watts Watts cargo liner service from East Canada to Europe replaced by the Wanstead class in 1949-50.

HP cylinder cover was smashed on passage Avonmouth to Freemantle and she put into Colombo to where a new cover was flown from the UK.

Sold to the Great Eastern Shipping Co. of Bombay in 1958 for £130,000 and renamed JAG MATE. Scrapped in Bombay 1963. [1]

SS TEDDINGTON was sunk by an E boat off Cromer on 17/9/41 on her second voyage and bound for London with a cargo of ammunition and war stores. She caught fire and grounded and was a total loss.[1]

Provisional trials carried out in River Tay due to War Time conditions.[6]

TSMV PRIAM

Dundee City Archives

TSMV PRIAM (later TSMV GLENORCHY) was built for the Alfred Holt shipping Company. She sustained severe weather damage during a North Atlantic gale 5/12/42. Tanks and cases containing aircraft fuselages on deck broke loose and collided with hatches. There was 32 feet of water in No2 hold. Madeira was reached in safety and the cargo re-stowed. She was bound for the Middle East with 10,000 tons of military equipment and was in great danger of foundering. The cargo shifted again and the ship was down by the head and the fore deck awash. The cargo was restowed at Freetown. The army authorities advised the captain that explosives which had been saturated could become dangerous in three weeks. The master continued to Suez judging he had time but was prohibited from entering the Canal and had to discharge outside.

Transferred to the Glen Line in 1948 and renamed GLENORCHY joining her sister ship BRECONSHIRE which had spent the war as aircraft carrier HMS ACTIVITY.

No2 hold took fire at Port Swettenham 9/3/1950 while bound Yokohama to London and continued to Penang with a hold smouldering containing about 1000 tons of rubber, cotton goods and wood. CO_2 was injected by firemen at Penang for two hours and the hold flooded to 10 feet extinguishing the fire. [1]

1939 Requisitioned by Admiralty on the stocks; Work Stopped.

1941 Admiralty decided to complete to original specification as cost to convert to Escort Carrier too great.

1942 Finally delivered to owners; Ocean S.S. Co. taken into service under original name.

1948 Transferred to Glen Line; Re named GLENORCHY.

1970 Reverted to Blue Funnel; Re named PHEMIUS.

1971 Broken up at Kaohsuing, Taiwan.[6]

Built 1941   **Yard No** 387

Specifications
10,029 Gross tons
475 x 66 x 38 feet

Machinery
Diesel twin 14,750 BHP total, by J G
Kincaid of Greenock
6cyl 620 dia 1400mm stroke
18 knots

Complement
68 Passengers   102 Crew

HMS ACTIVITY

HMS ACTIVITY was built as a cargo liner for the Alfred Holt shipping company but was taken over by the Admiralty on the stocks for conversion to an auxiliary aircraft carrier. Original name was TELEMACHUS and after WW2 was converted to the merchant vessel BRECONSHIRE.

Keel laid 1/2/40 as TELEMACHUS and progress was slow as Naval work given priority. Examined for conversion late 1941, aquired as an escort aircraft carrier in January 1942 and in service by October. One of a few British built escort carriers she was the heaviest ship launched in the Tay at that time. The flight deck was 492 feet and the overall dimensions were 512 x 66 x 26 feet.

Used for training Naval airmen in the West of Scotland during its first few months of service. In January 1944 she was in the Clyde for night flying exercises after a refit at Liverpool. On 29/1/44 she left the Clyde along with another merchant ship carrier HMS NAIRANA to support Captain F. Walker's U-boat hunter-killer group. Her aircraft were Wildcats and Swordfish. She was switched to two Halifax bound convoys and on Feb 4 -5 oiled Naval escort vessels. On March 27th she was called upon to assist a North Russian convoy, though not Arcticised*, with another carrier HMS TRECKER.

ACTIVITY's 7 Wildcats and 3 Swordfish concentrated on shadowing enemy aircraft and TRECKER dealt with the U-boats. 6 enemy aircraft were shot down by ACTIVITY's planes and ships of the convoy. On April 19th she left Scapa to escort a homeward bound Russian convoy and experienced difficulty with snow on the deck.

First public mention of ACTIVITY was on 25/4/44 being reported in action with U-boats in the Arctic Circle while escorting a convoy bound for Russia on 3/4/44.

Heavy weather was experienced and U-288 was sunk by ACTIVITY's aircraft.

Sent to the Far East in 1945 and used to ferry planes to the British East Indies and Pacific fleets. Sold to the Glen Line in 1946, converted for merchant service on the Tyne and renamed BRECONSHIRE. Sold to scrappers in 1967 for £140,000.[1]

1946 Purchased 'as lies' by Glen Line; Converted back to original design by Palmers Hebburn C. Ltd; Proceeded on commercial trials; Handed over as BRECONSHIRE. 1967 Broken Up at Kobe, Japan by Atak & Co. Ltd. Of Osaka.

*Insulation applied to inside the hull to retain heat and reduce condensation.

Built 1942	**Yard No** 388

Specifications
 11,462 Gross tons
 475 x 66 x 38 feet (as TELEMACHUS)

Machinery
Diesel twin 14750 BHP by J G Kincaid of Greenock
18 knots capable of 19.5knots

Complement
 0 Passengers   700 Crew

MV GOLD RANGER

Dundee City Archives

MV GOLD RANGER was built for the Admiralty Naval Stores Department as a fast tanker. Sister ships also built at the Caledon were GRAY RANGER and GREEN RANGER (pictured). The ship's capacities were 2600t oil fuel, 550t diesel and 90t petrol. They had the same engine power as 12,000 ton tankers and were therefore fast ships.

Employed mainly in the Far East after WW2 but did include trips to Hudson Bay and Antarctica. Scrapped at Hong Kong in 1977.[1]

GREY RANGER took part in the Lofotens raid 22-28 November 1941.

Torpedoed in the North Atlantic 22/9/42 convoy GP14 on return passage from N Russia. There were 21 survivors. [1]

GREEN RANGER was struck by a practice torpedo at Portland harbour in 1946 but damage was slight. Damaged in collision with tanker BUCCANEER 31/7/57 off Beachy Head and lost anchors and damaged forepeak. Wrecked at Hartland point north Devon 17/11/62.[1]

Built 1941   **Yard No** 389

Specifications
3313 Gross tons
335 x 48 x 22 feet

Machinery
Diesel 3150 IHP by Wm Doxford of Sunderland 2 stroke SA opposed piston 4Cyl 560mm dia 2160mm combined stroke 13 knots

Complement
 0 Passengers   47 Crew inc gunners

SS EMPIRE HEYWOOD

SS EMPIRE HEYWOOD was built for HM Ministry of Shipping. Sister ships also built at the Caledon were
EMPIRES: RHODES, PRINCE and ARCHER (see overleaf).

In 1946 EMPIRE HEYWOOD was used along with another ship to take 1500 illegal Jewish immigrants from
Haifa to Famagusta (Cyprus). On 18/8/46 an attempt was made to blow a hole in the ships side an explosion
taking place half an hour after leaving Haifa with 750 immigrants. Happily no casualties resulted. She was sold
to the Saint Line of London and renamed SAINT GREGORY. She survived several collisions and also ran out
of fuel off Malaysia 9/7/66. Scrapped at Hong Kong in 1967.[1]

Built 1941   **Yard No** 393

Specifications
 7029 Gross tons
 425 x 56 x 38 feet

Machinery
Steam triple expansion by NEM (1938)Ltd
of Wallsend
24.5 39 70/48   HP 220psi
11 knots

Complement
 0 Passengers   63 Crew inc gunners

EMPIRE RHODES, PRINCE, and ARCHER
(for photograph see previous page)

EMPIRE RHODES had a fire in its UNRRA* jute cargo at Gdynia Poland 18/12/45 after arrival from Calcutta. It was towed to the breakwater with 3 holds ablaze and settled with a 22 deg. List. It was refloated and set off for Kiel with two tugs.
Sold to the South Georgia company in 1946 and renamed CUTTER. Went Ashore entering Newcastle NSW in July 1955 carrying 9000 tons of ironstone and was refloated 9/7/55. Sold in 1959 to Pacific Warrior Shipping Co. of Liberia for £54,000 after being laid up for a year in the Holy Loch. Renamed VIRGINIA IPAR and sailed under the Turkish flag finally being scrapped at Istanbul after being laid up for seven years.[1]

EMPIRE PRINCE was sold to the Clan line for £144,800 in November 1945 and renamed CLAN ANGUS. Her propeller was lost 15 miles off Saugar, India when bound from Calcutta to Chittagong and was towed to Dumayne. A new tail shaft 19' 6" long and weighing 6.25 tons was flown out in the bomb bay of a Liberator this being a 3 day flight. Ship transferred to ownership of Ballard King & Co the Natal line under British and Commonwelth management and renamed UMKUZI. Worked the South African trade and was scrapped in Japan in 1962.[1]

EMPIRE ARCHER was managed by Raeburn and Varel Ltd 1942-6. Aground on mud in the Shat El Arab waterway 4/1/46. Ship sold to H Hogarth of Glasgow and renamed BARON MURRAY. At Dundee with 9000 tons of sugar in May 1949. Sold in July 1959 to the Cathay Pacific Shipping Corporation of Hong Kong for £72,500. Scrapped Yokohama Japan 1963.[1]
Fitted with 10x5 ton 1x30 tons and 1x50 tons S.W.L. Derricks.
1942 Sailed from Loch Ewe in Convoy JW51B as Commodore Vessel for Murmansk. Arrived Kola Inlet 3rd Jan 1943.
1943 Sailed from Kola Inlet in convoy RA53 for Loch Ewe Arrived Loch Ewe 14th March.
1944 Sailed from Loch Ewe in convoy JW63 [38 ships] as Vice Commodore,for Murmansk. This Convoy was undetected by the enemy, arrived at Kola Inlet.
1945 Sailed from Kola Inlet in convoy as Vice Commodore for Loch Ewe. This Convoy encountered very severe weather arrived in U.K. early March.
1946 To Kelvin Shipping Co., Ltd., Glasgow; Re named BARON MURRAY. Port of registry Ardrossan; H. Hogarth & Sons Managers.
1950 Converted to burn Oil Fuel.[6]

*United Nations Relief and Rehabilitation Administration.

SS EMPIRE BARD

SS EMPIRE BARD was built for HM Ministry of Shipping for timber carrying duties.
She was a standard Scandinavian design of 4700 tons deadweight designed by Wm Gray & Co of Hartlepool who built 48 of them. Managed by the Currie Line. Equipped with heavy derricks for discharging tanks in Russian ports without heavy shore cranes. She survived many air attacks in convoy to North Russia. Reached port and remained there 10 months during which there were air attacks without respite.
During one attack a near miss caused a fire in the magazine and William Hadley AB took a hose into the magazine and put out the fire. He Received Lloyds war medal as did captain Henry Soalmans. Ship sold to DP&L in July 1946, with derricks and winches removed, for £74,500 and renamed ANGUSBURN. Changed ownership several times as BRETTENHAM and was scrapped at Carthagena, Spain in 1971.[1]

Sailed from Oban in Convoy PQ 14 [having sailed from Dundee in loaded condition] for Reykjavik & Murmansk. Encountered 30 hrs of fog and heavy pack ice forcing her to return to Iceland. Sailed from Reyjavik in Convoy PQ 14 for Murmansk Remained in this area as 'Crane Ship'. Worked between Murmansk and Archangel as required.
1943 Brought cranes of English Construction [Cargo] from Archangel to Murmansk.
Aug.28th left Kola Inlet in convoy RA59A. Arrived Loch Ewe 5th Sept.
1946 Sold to Dundee, Perth & London Shipping co., Ltd., Dundee; Renamed ANGUSBURN heavy gear now removed; purchase price £74,500.
1951 Converted to Oil fuel on Tyneside cost nearly £20,000.
1954 To Brebner Shipping Co., Ltd., London; Renamed BRETTENHAM ; Signal Letters GIFA; Price £90,000
1955 To Rederi A/B Hildeguaard, Mariehamn, Finland; name Unchanged; Port of Registry Mariehamn; Price £130,000 Signal Letters OFVB.
1971 Arrived at Cartagena, Spain for breaking up; Demolition commenced by Francisco Jimenez Ballester[6]

Built 1941	**Yard No** 396

Specifications
3113 Gross tons
310 x 46 x 25 feet

Machinery
Steam triple expansion 1200 IHP by NEM of Newcastle
20 31 55/39   HP 200 psi
10 knots

Complement
0 Passengers   43 Crew inc gunners

MV TELEMACHUS

MV TELEMACHUS was built for the Alfred Holt shipping Company the earlier ship of the same name being converted to HMS ACTIVITY.

In 1956 she was the first ship to sail into Tsingtao under the Chinese Communist Regime. Suffered machinery breakdown off Semarang , Java 8/5/56. taken in tow by TANTALUS arriving in Surabaya 11/5/56. Ship and cargo valued at £677,440. A friendly action was held in the Admiralty court to assess salvage awards. Capt F W Curphey of TANTALUS was awarded £800 and the crew of 56 got £1,800.

Transferred to the Blue Funnel line in 1963 and renamed GLOUCUS.

Sold for scrap in 1968 for £121,000.[1]

Trials on River Tay.

A Holt & Co.,Managers.

1957 Transferred to Glen Line; Renamed MONMOUTHSHIRE; Port of registry Liverpool.

1963 Chartered to China Navigation Co., [John Swire & sons]; Renamed NANCHANG. Port of registry unchanged.

1968 Broken up at Hong Kong by Leung Yao Ship Breakers.[6]

Built 1943	**Yard No** 397

Specifications
 8262 Gross tons
 452 x 61 x 35 feet

Machinery
Diesel 8500 BHP by JG Kincaid of Greenock
8 cyl 620mm dia 1400 stroke
15 knots

Complement
13 Passengers 75 Crew 19 DEMS gunners

SS ASCOT

At ASCOT .. launch.

SS ASCOT was built for the Watts Watts shipping company of London.
The engines were designed for superheat and reheat but were installed for saturated steam in wartime conditions. The coal consumption tons/day stated were 32.5 saturated., 27.5 superheat., 23.5 reheat.[2]
Launched during a SW gale the tugs could not control her and she grounded in front of the shipyard with the nose over the end of the slipway. Damage was sustained forward and she was floated the following day.
Torpedoed in the Indian Ocean while sailing alone on voyage from Colombo to Diego Saurez, Madagascar. The ship began to sink quickly but the crew got away in the boats. The submarine surfaced and shelled the ship and rammed the boats and rafts and machined the occupants. All but 8 were killed. The Captain was taken aboard the Japanese submarine for questioning then thrown overboard. Survivors picked up 3 days later by Dutch Merchant ship. Apprentice Harry Fortune was awarded the Lloyds War medal for courage and resource in keeping a boat afloat with survivors including wounded and responsible for the 8 being rescued.[1]

Built 1942	**Yard No** 398

Specifications
7004 Gross tons
410 x 56 x 28 feet

Machinery
Steam triple expansion 2000 IHP by NEM of Wallsend
23.5 38 66/45　　　　　　　　HP 220
10.5 knots
Complement
0 Passengers 46 Crew 20 DEMS gunners

MV TARKWA

Dundee City Archives

MV TARKWA was built for the Elder Dempster shipping line.
During 1945 she averaged 13.25 knots on voyage Calcutta to Dundee with jute carrying 40 first class and 32 second class passengers. On fire at Liverpool 24/8/45 where 1000 bales of cotton were damaged. Afire at Liverpool 5/6/63 for 1.5 hours.
Sold to the Golden Line of Singapore for £115,000 in 1967 and the Singapore Maritime flag was hoisted for the first time when the ship was taken over in the Thames. Renamed GOLDEN LION. Grounded at Batu Berkanti off Singapore 16/1/71. Sold to Chinese breakers arriving at Shanghai May 1971.[1]

1967 Sold to Guan Guan Shipping [Pte] Ltd., Singapore for £115,000; Renamed GOLDEN LION Port of Registry Singapore.
1971 Sold to Chinese mainland Shipbreakers; Arrived Shanghai for demolition by China National Machinery Import and Export Company.[6]

"I was browsing through your 'reminiscing' page, and a memory came back to me of around 1958 when I was a young apprentice on a ship named 'Tarkwa' belonging to Elder Dempster's of Liverpool. We did one of many voyages to West Africa but what was special on this ship was that we had our own jazz band. Apart from playing on the ship we entertained in a number of places ashore, most notably, (in my memory at least), for a 'Ladies Night' dance at the Port Harcourt European Club in Nigeria." Richard Knock [Jazzworld web site].

Built 1943	**Yard No** 399

Specifications
 7416 Gross tons
 425 x 39 x 56 feet

Machinery
Diesel 5400 BHP by J G Kincaid of Greenock 4 stroke SA
8cyl 740mm Dia 1500 mm stroke.
14 knots

Complement
40Passengers 70Crew 12 DEMS gunners

SS Scottish Monarch (2)

SS SCOTTISH MONARCH was built for the Monarch Shipping Co. of Glasgow. {Sister ship NORMAN MONARCH (pictured) built about the same time}.

Under command of Captain H J M Downie of Freuchie as a brand new ship; she took part in military operations at Sicily, Salerno, Greece and South of France.

Aground at Cape Cod Canal 15/5/45 causing steering gear damage which was not discovered till Alexandria 19/6/45. She struck a wreck near Bizerta in 1946 on passage Taltal to Alexandria with 9271 tons of Nitrate and was beached. Loaded esparto grass for Glasgow where repairs were carried out costing £120,000; converted from coal to oil burning at this time. Fire in No 1 hold while in the Bay of Biscay 5/3/54 en route from Liverpool to West Africa with matches in the cargo. She put back to Plymouth with the hold steam smothered. Discharged damaged cargo including 32 tons matches, 10 tons sugar, 84 tons stout and 10 tons general cargo.

Sold to Red Pantics A/B Abo in1957 for £235,000 renamed RAGNI PAULIN. Sold to Chinese breakers 1969. [1]

Raeburn & Verel,Managers. 1947 Returned to Dundee for conversion from coal to oil fuel.

Sold to Eastern Seafaring & Trading Co., S.A. Panama for £465,000. Renamed DEMETRIUS DS Port of Registry Panama.

1958 to Hemisphere Shipping Co., Ltd.,Hong Kong the Hong Kong agents for The Chinese People's Republic. Sold for £130,000 after eight month lay up in Rotterdam. Several name changes.

1967 Renamed ZHAN DOU Port of Registry Shanghai. Same Owners.

Still Listed as above L.R. 1983-84-85.

L.R: Owners Government of the People's Republic of China; [Bureau of Maritime Transport Administration-Shangai Branch] [6]

Built 1943   **Yard No** 401

Specifications
 7004 Gross tons
 425 x 56 x 27 feet

Machinery
Steam triple expansion 2500 IHP by
Fairfields of Glasgow
24.5 39 70/48   HP 220 psi
10.5 knots

Complement
 0 Passengers   55 Crew inc gunners

SS LAPLAND

Dundee City Archives

SS LAPLAND (sister ship ICELAND also Caledon built) was built for the Currie line of Leith.
She was fitted with heavy lifting derricks for handling tanks the derricks being removed after the war. Returned to Caledon for coal to oil conversion May 1948.
Fire in stokehold at Victoria Dock Dundee 20/5/48 caused by welder's torch igniting diesel oil. In collision in the Mersey 28/5/49 causing bows and plates damage costing £2000. Struck by Royal Mail Line ship DARRO in a gale at Swansea 23/3/55. On fire at St John's Newfoundland 24/9/55. Grounded at Laago Fiord, Scheldt, Lagos. Laid up at London 12/57 and moved to Burntisland 6/58.
Sold at London to Greek owners for £53,000 in 1959 to sail under Panama flag .
Owners Halcophil Beyrouth of Lebanon renamed HARSTAD. Damaged in collision at Iskenderun 17/4/62. Engineroom fire 1/2/67 extinguished and the ship proceeded to Bizerta. Renamed LEANA in 1968. Scrapped 1973.[1]
Engined by North Eastern Marine; Fitted with heavy lift gear for handling tanks and transferring heavy lifts at North Russian Ports. Including 2-80 ton S.W.L derricks on specially strengthened posts and also 8-5 ton S.W.L derricks. In 1944 she sailed from Loch Ewe in convoy JW61 arriving at Kola Inlet on Oct 28th. Very strong escort, no losses.
In 1945 she remained working in this area,and did not leave for U.K. until post Aug. 1945. Heavy lift gear and derrick posts (2) were removed.
1957 laid up at London and in 1958 Moved to Burntisland. In 1959 sold to Halcophil Campania Naveira S.A. Lebanon for £53,000; Renamed PAVLOS Port of Registry Beirut (Bayrouth).
1967 Renamed LEANA under the same owners; Managers c/o Victoria S.S.Co.,Ltd., London.E.C.2 port of Registry Lebanon. 1973 Broken up at Piraeus.
Sistership to ICELAND which had 1943 yard no 403 similar to "Scandinavian" type built to Ministry of Shipping [later Ministry of War Transport] specifications.[6]

Built 1942	**Yard No** 402

Specifications
 2897 Gross tons
 310 x 46 x 25 feet

Machinery
Steam triple expansion 1200 IHP by NEM
of Wallsend
20 31 59/39   HP 200psi
10 knots
Complement
 Passengers   Crew 49 inc 10 gunners

SS EMPIRE CAPTAIN

SS EMPIRE CAPTAIN was built for HM Ministry of Shipping. Sister ships of this class namely EMPIRE KITCHENER, EMPIRE LIFE and SS TERBORCH for the Dutch Government were also built by the Caledon S&E at this time.

First of seven 15 knot high class cargo liners carrying 30 passengers. Sold to Canadian Pacific in February 1946 for the Liverpool-London-East Canada service and renamed BEAVERBURN. First ship of the season at Montreal 21/4/47 and Captain J B Smith received a gold mounted cane. In collision off Quebec 17/6/47 with schooner St Joseph which was abandoned but later towed in. BEAVERBURN and BEAVERFORD carried 1295 passengers in 1947 (passenger accommodation reduced from 35 to 12 in 1948 and discontinued in 1953).

Sold to Ben Line for £140,000 in 1960 and renamed BENACHIE. Suffered an engineroom fire at Singapore 2/7/60 and crew abandoned ship in the early morning because of threatened explosion from 60 boxes of detonators stored in a hold next to the engineroom. The crew flooded the engineroom prior to leaving and the blaze was subdued after three hours when the crew reboarded and threw the detonators overboard. Sold to Taiwan owners for £158,000 sailing under a Liberian flag and renamed SILVANA .[1]

T.& J. Harrisons,Managers; Trial run on Arran Mile.

Sold in 1964 To Atlantic Navigation Corporation Ltd., Liberia; Renamed SILVANA Price £158,000   Port of Registry Monrovia.

1969 sold to Outerocean Navigation Co., Ltd., Taiwan; Name unchanged; Port of Registry Kaihsiung.

1971 to Ming Kang Steel Enterprise Ltd., began demolition at Kaohsiung.[6]

Built 1944	**Yard No** 404

Specifications
9874 Gross tons
 465 x 64 x 43 feet

Machinery
Steam turbine 6800 SHP by Richardsons
Westgarth HP 430psi
15 knots

Complement
35 Passengers
Crew 94 inc 13gunners 4 radar

SS TERBORCH
Ship image and details as SS EMPIRE CAPTAIN

Yard No 405 1944. Sold to the Holland America Line in 1946 and renamed EERNDIJK on the Holland-London-Gulf of Mexico trade. In a storm in the North Atlantic 30/1/50 en route Rotterdam to New Orleans when deck cargo of heavy steel bars broke loose and fell into a hold damaging the shaft tunnel and disabled the ship which was towed to Rotterdam.
Sold for £150,000 to the Orient Middle East Line of Panama under a Greek flag and renamed ORIENT MERCHANT. She was in the Great Lakes 1964-5 with grain for relief organizations and was trapped in the ice at Toronto with three other ships.
In 1965 she was ordered back to Chicago to load more cargo for the Far East. Delay experienced in getting through the Welland canal due to pack ice. In 1965 she was stranded at Port Calbourne with serious bottom damage requiring 70 plates to be replaced. Under arrest for $13,000 owing to the Great Lakes Salvage company.
In 1965 sold in Canada and resold to Liberia having been declared a constructive total loss. Renamed ZAMBEZI in Labrador and sailed to the Gulf in damaged condition to load grain for the Med. Left Toronto 17/9/65. Grounded in Hooghly off Kidderpore with grain from Galveston. Sold to Formosa breakers 1967.[1]

SS EMPIRE KITCHENER
Ship image and details as SS EMPIRE CAPTAIN

Sold to the Canadian Pacific Steamship Co. in 1946 being renamed BEAVERFORD.
Brought an emergency shipment of 2800 tons of potatoes to Cardiff during a shortage in the UK. Trapped in the ice at Montreal in December 1958 and not freed till January. Plates were damaged and pipes frozen. Stuck for 4 hours in London Docks in the Albert dock lockway. Sold to Monrovian owners 1966 and renamed HULDA. Damaged during hurricane Camille in August 1969 after collision with several ships resulting in serious damage. Abandoned as a constructive total loss in October 1969. Stranded at Gulfport and demolished on the spot.

EMPIRE LIFE
Ship image and details as SS EMPIRE CAPTAIN

Sold to the Union Castle Line in April 1946. Sold to Union Castle Line April 1946 and renamed GOOD HOPE CASTLE and started a Cape – USA service. It was the first Union Castle liner to be registered in the Union. When the company entered a 10 year mail contract in 1945 it agreed that 20% of personnel on each ship would be U of SA nationals and that ship repairs would be done in South Africa.
Engine trouble en route SA to UK in 1951. Stopped at Aden and left for UK at reduced speed. Repaired at Belfast. Sold to Hong Kong breakers in1959 for £80,000.

SS EMPIRE CANYON

SS EMPIRE CANYON was built for HM Ministry of Shipping.
Managers Strick Line Ltd.
1947 To Alexander Shipping Co., Ltd.,(Capper,A. Alexander & Co.,Houlder Bros., & Co., Ltd.,); Renamed
HOLMBURY Port of Register London; Price £170,000
1960 To United General Shipping Co., Karachi; Renamed ILYASBAKSH Port of Registry Karachi. Price
£95,000.
1965 Arrived at Bombay; placed under restraint whilst undergoing rudder repairs ;Pakistan-Indian War.
1966 Impounded by Indian Government. Classed LR until 3/67.
1970 Scrapped at Bombay by Najabali & Co.[6]

Built 1943	**Yard No** 408

Specifications
7058 Gross tons
425 x 56 x 29 feet

Machinery
Steam triple expansion 2050 IHP by NEM
of Wallsend
24.5 39 70/48   HP 220 psi
11 knots

Complement
 0 Passengers   Crew 66 inc gunners

MV RHEXENOR

Dundee City Archives

MV RHEXENOR and sister ship MV STENTOR were built for the China Mutual steam navigation Co.,managers Alfred Holt Shipping Co of Liverpool.
Employed mainly in the UK-Australian trade. In 1958 took a 117 ton decarbonising tower as deck cargo from Glasgow to Australia. This was 56 feet high and intended for the Kurnell refinery near Sydney. The tower was discharged over the side and floated to the refinery. In 1975 she was renamed HERENO. Sold to Tiawan breakers in 1975.[1]
The owners usually had a "standby" engineer and deck officer from their staff to witness and advise during the ship's construction. The engineer on RHEXENOR and STENTOR was the notable Lady Marine Engineer Victoria Drummond of Megginch Castle Errol, Perthshire, who had served her apprenticeship at the Caledon Engineworks, Lilybank Foundry, completing it in the early 1920's. [5]

MV STENTOR sister ship to RHEXENOR was also for the UK-Australia trade. In 1948 outward bound from the UK she towed the TROILUS of the same owners when it lost its propeller 1016 miles to Aden. The accident occurred to Troilus 420 miles SE of Socotra. STENTOR was 550 miles away off cape Guardefui when contact was made by radar. Troilus had drifted 100 miles NE with the monsoon blowing and conditions difficult. Under tow 70 miles were made on the worst day and 226 miles on the best making Aden on 12th July. GLENOGIL took the tow from Aden 4365 miles to the UK. STENTOR was awarded £18,000 in the Admiralty court and GLENOGIL £22,000 with masters and crews getting 33% of the total. The master received 3/7 and the crew 4/7 of the STENTOR'S 6,000.
Transferred to the Glen line in 1958 as GLENSHIEL and retransferred in 1968 to the Blue Funnel line renamed STENTOR. She took a 79 ton cased turbine by John Browns from Glasgow to Bangkok for the Bon Kapi power station. Renamed TENTO in 1995 and sold to Kaiohsiung, Taiwan, breakers .[1]

Built 1945	**Yard No** 409

Specifications
10,199 Gross tons
465 x 64 x 43 feet

Machinery
Diesel 7500BHP by J G Kincaid of Greenock 8cyl Dia 550mm 1600 combined stroke, 2 stroke opposed piston.
15 knots

Complement
36 Passengers   Crew 76

81

SS EMPIRE FAVOUR

SS EMPIRE FAVOUR (sister ship MV EMPIRE CANNING also built at Caledon) was built for HM Ministry of Shipping to be managed by Messrs Clark and Service of Glasgow. She was sold in 1947 to the Britain Steamship Co. (Watts Watts) and renamed EPSOM then sold in 1950 to the United British Steamship Co. (Holdin & Co.) for £112,000 and renamed ERRINGTON COURT.

In 1956 she was sold to Ciade Nav Hellepoint of Panama for £400,000 and renamed PENELOPE. She was sold to Greek owners in Pireus in 1964 and renamed ANDROMACHI. On 25/6/69 she was hit by Israeli shells at Suez during a 5 hour artillery battle across the Suez canal the resulting fire aboard lasting several hours.

The fire was extinguished by the Egyptians the engine room and bridge being gutted.

She was abandoned and the crew repatriated the ship being towed to Hurghadi at the entry to the Gulf of Suez where openings were to be closed. In 1974 the fire damaged hulk was still aground South of Adabiyo. The canal was in the process of clearance after closure for several years. She was sold for scrap and the process started in March 1976.[1]

In 1976 as ANDROMACHI she was broken up near Suez at Adabiyah by Hosin Abdel Aziz.[6]

Built 1945	**Yard No** 411

Specifications
7056 Gross tons
425 x 56 x 38 feet

Machinery
Steam triple expansion   2500 IHP by
Duncan Stewart of Glasgow
24.5 39 70/48   HP 220 psi
11 knots

Complement
0 Passengers   56 Crew

MV EMPIRE CANNING

Dundee City Archives

MV EMPIRE CANNING was built for HM Ministry of Shipping (managers H Hogarth Glasgow). (Sister ship to EMPIRE FAVOUR but with diesel engine.)

During the Indonesian troubles she was at Surabaya on 15/11/45 where six shells from a 75mm gun landed close to the ship, the nearest being 20 yards away. She was sold in 1946 to the Britain Steamship Co (Watts Watts) and renamed WILLESDEN later being involved in a collision in London Docks in 1947. There was a serious fire on board on 12/2/48 off South Australia en route from Adelaide to Palestine with 9000 tons of flour. The ship was anchored off Althorpe Islands with the engineroom ablaze and although the fire was critical it was fought by the crew with success and she was towed smouldering to Adelaide on 14/2/48. Steam was injected to quell the fire in the flour and over 2000 tons were ruined the overall damage amounting to £100,000. The ship was valued at £260,000 and cargo £440,000.

She was sold to the Worldwide Shipping Co. of Hong Kong in 1960 and renamed MARINE EXPLORER. Sold in 1962 to the Viking Shipping Co. of Hong Kong and renamed EAST VIM. Renamed again in 1963 as WAKASABY and in 1965-6 was blacklisted by the US Government for trading with North Vietnam. Also she was banned from US ports and from taking US cargoes to other countries. Placed on charter to Japan the owners stopped Vietnam trading immediately. Transferred in 1966 to Leo Steamship Co. of Hong Kong she was renamed GOLDEN WIND and later broken up in 1967.[1]

1966 Arrived at Wakayama for breaking up by Mitsui & Co., Ltd., Japan; Demolition began at Tsuneishi-cho Hiroshima. [6]

Built 1944	**Yard No** 412

Specifications
 6996 Gross tons
 425 x 56 x 38 feet

Machinery
Diesel 3300 IHP by Hawthorn Leslie
(Werkspoor)
Cyl 8 x 550   Stroke 1200mm
12 knots

Complement
0 Passengers   Crew 91 incl 11 gunners

HMS CARISBROOKE CASTLE

Corvette HMS CARISBROOKE CASTLE and sister ships DUMBARTON CASTLE and HURST CASTLE were built for the British Admiralty. These Castle Class Corvettes were a much improved vessel to the Flower class Corvettes. The improved length designed by William Reed of Smith's Dock made these more suitable for Atlantic Weather conditions.

Launched 31/7/43 1943 she was delivered on 17/11/43. In 1946 she was placed on fishery protection duties in the North Sea being refitted at Penarth in 1949. Scrapped in 1958 at Shipbreaking Industries of Faslane where the process took 8 weeks. Stanislav Zavradsta cut the ship into sections suitable for lifting ashore for other burners reduced them to blast furnace size scrap. Engines for DUMBARTON CASTLE were by Hick Hargreaves and those for HURST CASTLE by Thorneycroft. Dumbarton Castle was scrapped at Gateshead in 1960 and HURST CASTLE was torpedoed, with loss of life, near Tory island off NW Ireland 1/9/44 on her maiden voyage.[1]

HMS CARISBROOKE CASTLE Pendant Nos. K379, F379.[6]

Built 1943 **Yard No** 414

Specifications
1369 Gross tons 1060 tons Dispacement
225 x 36 x 17 feet

Machinery
Steam triple 2880 IHP by Geo Clark
18.5 knots

Complement
0 Passengers   121 Crew

HMS LOCH LOMOND

The Lochs were based upon the hull of the preceding River class with increased sheer and flare to improve seakeeping and modified to suit it to mass pre-fabrication, with sections riveted or welded together at the shipyard. Accordingly, as many curves as possible were eliminated, producing a noticeable kink in the main deck where the increased sheer forwards met the level abreast the bridge.[Loch class website]

Frigate HMS LOCH LOMOND (sister ship to HMS LOCH MORE (pictured)) was built for the British Admiralty.
This was an anti-submarine frigate launched on 19/6/44 and completed 16/11/44.
Taken from the reserve and sent to the Med in April 1950 to replace a destroyer.
Scrapped at Faslane 1969. [1]
Delivered to Admirality Pendant No. K437.
Ran Trials off Firth of Tay Speed 18.919 knots.
1969 Broken up at Faslane, Gareloch. [6]

HMS LOCH MORE As LOCH LOMOND but engines were by Blairs Ltd. Laid down 16/3/44 she was delivered 24/2/45. Along with HMS LOCH GLENDHU she attacked and heavily damaged a U boat off Northern Scotland early in 1945. After the crew had abandoned the U boat a party from LOCH MORE boarded the sub and attempted a tow however the U boat sank. Temporary midshipman J R Watson RNR leader of the boarding party was awarded the MBE for courage and initiative..On Mediterranean service 1950. Scrapped by T W Ward at Inverkiething 1963. [1]
Pendant No. K639; Speed on trials 10.01 knots.
1963 Broken up by T.W, Ward, Inverkeithing.[6]

Built 1944 **Yard No** 417

Specifications
1888 Gross tons 1435 tons Dispacement

286 x 38 x 18 feet

Machinery
Twin Steam triple expansion (4 cyl) by
Duncan Stewart of Glasgow
18.5 31 38.5 38.5/30 6500 IHP
HP 200 psi   Twin screw
19.5 knots

Complement   136 Crew

HMS LOCH TRALAIG

HMS LOCH TRALAIG (sister ship to LOCH ARKAIG (pictured)) was laid down 26/6/44 and delivered 7/7/45. Along with frigates LOCH ARKAIG, FADA and DUNVEGAN formed the anti-submarine school at Londonderry in January 1946. Fleet Air Arm and RAF aircraft co-operated using Battle of the Atlantic airports Bally Kelly and Castle Archdale.

She took part in North Sea maneouvres from Rosyth, Fife in May 1948. Scrapped at T & W McLellan of Bo'Ness 1963.[1]

HMS LOCH ARKAIG Delivered to Admiralty 1945. Pendant No K 603.
1960 Broken Up by J.J.King, Gateshead, River Tyne.[6]

Built 1945 Yard Nos 420 & 421

Specifications
1888 Gross tons 1435 tons Dispacement

286 x 38 x 18 feet

Machinery
Twin steam turbines by BTH Ltd double reduction geared, two shafts Twin screw
HP 220 psi
19.5 knots

Complement
0 Passengers   136 Crew

MV MODJOKERTO

Dundee City Archives

MV MODJOKERTO was a cargo liner built for Rotterdam Lloyd. This ship was comprehensively photographed at her completion suggesting that it was a new design incorporating post war ideas and finishes.

On 6/6/58 the ship, with 36 passengers aboard, went ashore near Tondjong Meni anchorage Indonesia where it was to load timber but was towed off undamaged after 1000 tons of water ballast pumped out. Sold to Greek owners Socrates Navigation Co. SA Panama 1963 for £130,000 and renamed DONA RITA. Sold in 1968 to South Korean Atlas Line of Inchon. Renamed ATLAS PROMOTER.
In 1971 she was sold to Hyundi International Inc. Inchon. Placed on charter at $1050 per day at 14.5 knots on the British Columbia – Singapore run via the Red Sea and East Africa (Sovereign Marine). Sold to Taiwan breakers 1972.[1]

Built 1946   **Yard No** 422

Specifications
10,154 Gross tons
 465 x 64 x 43 feet

Machinery
Diesel 6800 BHP by Kincaid/Harland & Wolff
Cyl 8 x 550   stroke 1200mm 2stroke
15 knots

Complement
30 Passengers   69 Crew

MV ANCHISES

Dundee City Archives

MV ANCHISES was built for Alfred Holt & Co. She was bombed and machine gunned when approaching Shanghai about 9am in good visibility on 21/6/49 and was beached on Gough Island Astree channel Whangpoo river. The engine room was flooded and the ship took a 9 degree list.The aircraft was a P51 belonging to the Central Government Air Force. (Shanghai had been occupied by the Communists).

Four crew were injured. She was attacked again on the 22nd June but was refloated and beached at Shanghai. The Far east freight conference suspended sailings to Shanghai. The National Government apologized and undertook to compensate in accord with international law. The tug CAROLINE MOLLER towed ANCHISES to Kobe, Japan for repairs. Repairs cost £200,000. In 1969 11 Seddon buses 32 feet long and weighing 6 tons each were loaded at Liverpool for Hong Kong.

In 1970 Captain James Ray of 91 Dalhousie Road Barnhill was detained by the Chinese authorities at Shanghai for alleged breach of harbour regulations. The charge related to the marking of positions of buoys. The ship sailed for Singapore on 5/3/70 in charge of the chief officer. Captain Ray was detained for almost three weeks. The second officer of MV GLENFALLOCH was detained at the same time on similar charges. Both signed "confessions" but were not ill treated and reached London on 29/3/70. The Ocean group suspended all sailings to Shanghai as a result.

In 1972 she was renamed ALCINIOUS and went to the breakers in 1975.[1]

1974 Transferred to Glen Line; then reverted to China Mutual S.N. Co.

1975 Arrived Kaohsiung for breaking up.[6]

Built 1946	**Yard No** 423

Specifications
8286 Gross tons
450 x 62 x 35 feet

Machinery
Diesel 2 stroke   6800 BHP by G J Kincaid
(Harland B&W)
Cyl 8 x 550mm   Stroke 1200mm
15 knots

Complement
12 Passengers   72 Crew

MV SZECHUEN

MV SZECHUEN was built for John Swire & Co. Employed on the Hong Kong to Keelung service carrying 89 passengers and freight. On 7/9/1963 she was quarantined at Keelung having arrived there with 118 passengers and crew with two cases of cholera suspected but not confirmed. In 1966 she was sold to Selaton Enterprises of London (Kie Hock Shipping Hong Kong Ltd) for £160,000 and renamed TONG HIN.
In 1967 sold to the Africa Shipping Co. and renamed GAMBARIS.
In 1968 sold to the Karingo Shipping Co. and renamed KARINGO.
Sold in 1978 for demolition at Ming Hing Co. of Junk Bay Hong Kong .[1]

Built 1946   **Yard No** 424

Specifications
3033 Gross tons
298 x 46 x 25 feet

Machinery
Diesel 2 stroke SA 1750 BHP by Sulzer
Cyl 4 x 600mm   Stroke 1040mm

11.5 knots

Complement
89 Passengers   nd Crew

MV SCOTLAND

MV SCOTLAND was built for the Currie Line of Leith. Built for the Mediterranean trade she was launched as the SHETLAND but took the new name after a barge was renamed SCOTLAND II. Aground on the Shingles sands in the Thames in October 1960 en route Genoa to London. In December 1961 she brought the first cargo of Dry Martini in bulk to London carried in 70 containers containing 35,368 gallons. In collision in fog in the Thames 22/1/66 with the Spanish MV MARIMAR .

Sold to Greek owners L. Goudeles & others of Piraeus in 1967, renamed ELEFTHERIC and on her first voyage with superphosphate she hit a rocky bottom.

On 7/10/67 she was aground 30 miles east of Lagos en route Angola to Lagos. She dragged over an old wreck and was damaged aft. Sitting on a sandy bottom she was rounded by surf on Post side. Ground tackle was brought overland by Land Rover from Lagos and her head heaved round and seaward. Salvage was jeopardized by the defection of the engineroom staff but she refloated and was towed to Lagos.

In 1970 renamed DYROS under new Piraeus ownership and in 1974 renamed again ALEXANDRIA K. She was abandoned in the eastern Med 18/9/76 bound Eleusis to Jeddah with timber which caught fire. Reboarded and towed but abandoned a second time and lost presumed sunk.[1]

(See reference to SCOTLAND in the ENGLAND speech page 97).

Built 1945	**Yard No** 425

Specifications
2271 Gross tons
315 x 46 x 28 feet

Machinery
Diesel 2000 BHP by Kincaid of Greenock
4 Cyl Dia 630mm   Stroke 1300mm
12 knots

Complement
0 Passengers   37 Crew

TSMV RAJAH BROOKE

TSMV RAJAH BROOKE was built for the Sarawak Steamship Co.
She was designed in a Japanese wartime prison camp by Fred Ritchie, a native of Dundee, and was a shallow draught mail steamer for the Singapore–Kuching run sailing alternate Saturdays. 23/8/1967 she was aground at Labuan and refloated without damage. Transferred to the Straits steamship company (parent) in 1964 for the Borneo service. Scrapped in Singapore in 1980.[1]
Classed (Lloyds) for East Indian Archipeligo Service.
1964 Straits Shipping Pte., Ltd Singapore.
1980 Sold to National Shipbreakers Pty. Ltd., Singapore Commenced Demolition.[6]

Built 1947   **Yard No** 426

Specifications
 2311 Gross tons
425 x 56 x 38 feet

Machinery
Diesel Twin 1920 BHP by Polar Atlas of Glasgow
Cyls Dia 340mm Stroke 570mm

13 knots

Complement
40 1st Cl, 249 deck Passengers   78 Crew

91

TSMV TOWARD

TSMV TOWARD was built for the Clyde Shipping Co. Identical sister ships BEACHY, COPELAND and GODWIN were also built during the period 1946-8.

Her stem was damaged in a collision with SS ZELO at Purfleet 25/2/47 and at Greenwich in 18/4/53 with MV SWALLOW.

She was sold in 1962 for £85,000 to the Ionian SS Co of Greece in 1962 and renamed EPIROS. In 1965 she was renamed NEW EPIROTOKI of Potomionos Lines of Piraeus, and altered to carry 233 passengers in three classes.

On 7/3/69 she was stranded leaving Rhodes resulting in 18 plates damaged.

In 1969 she was being used as a drive on ferry for 40 cars and 2 coaches and 114/54/142 passengers in 3 classes on the Brindisi-Piraeus-Rhodes-Cyprus-Haifa run. Wrecked on Spyros Island 20/1/70 on a shelving beach where she caught fire and was gutted resulting in a total loss.[1]

Ran Trials off Tay Estuary.

1962 Ionian Steamship Navigation Co.,Ltd. Of Piraeus [Part of Potamianos Group]; Reconstructed as Cargo Passenger Ferry; Re named EPIROS Port of Registry Piraeus. Class suspended 10/62.[6]

Built 1946	Yard No 427
Specifications	
1271 Gross tons	
235 x 38 x 18 feet	
Machinery	
Diesel Twin 1920BHP total by British Polar of Glasgow (Atlas)	
2 x 6 Cyls Dia 340 Stroke 570mm	
13 knots	
Complement	
0 Passengers 22 Crew	

TSMV BEACHY

It was the custom for there to be a celebratory lunch or tea in the Caledon boardroom following the launch of a ship which was normally carried out by a lady.

The adjoining picture is of the Caledon Managing director Henry Main speaking at the lunch for the BEACHY; the lady on his right would be the one launching the ship. There would be other speeches e.g. by the owner's representative. See later the speech at the launch of the ENGLAND.

The plaque showing the Caledon founder Mr W B Thompson can be seen behind and the boardroom wall was a picture gallery of past Caledon built ships. The roof of the boardroom was a beautiful circular dome of stained glass with daylight shining through.

Ship's image is as TSMV TOWARD.

TSMV BEACHY was built for the Clyde Shipping Co. In 1959 she was on an African voyage to Mauritius and Durban. Sold to Yugoslavian owners Kvarners in 1959 and renamed SNJEZRUK. Capsized and sank in 25ft at Suda Bay harbour Crete 9/1/60 en route Haifa to Copenhagen with 900 tons of oranges and 100 tons olive oil. Lying on her starboard side she was refloated on March 26 and towed to Jugoslavia for repairs. Ashore on rocks with a 10 degree list to port on 5/12/60 at Famagusta Cyprus while assisting the Japanese liner NAGATU MARU, also aground.

RAF helicopter took off 18 crew and 6 others however one helicopter crashed but its crew were saved. The master still on board radioed that the ship was breaking up and the list had increased to 20 degrees. The cargo was timber and general for Famagusta and Haifa. Explosives and suction dredging were used to clear a path to deep water and the ship refloated on 29/4/61. She was sold to Italian breakers in 1961 and realized £17,500 as she lay at Famagusta. She left on 31/8/61 for Demolmere SPC Genoa but was resold to Panama flag in 1962 and renamed MAHA owners Reefer Navigation Company. In 1962 owned by Abughazelah of Kuwait. Aground near Freeport Bahamas 14/10/64 but refloated and towed to Genoa arriving 29/12/64. In July1966 MAHA put in to Singapore en route Freemantle to Persian Gulf with refrigerated cargo and livestock. Abandoned sinking off Trivendrum S.India October 1968 bound Singapore to Basrah with timber. 19 of crew picked up by Indian liner STATE of RAJISTAN.[1]

Other details as for TSMV TOWARD

MV ACHILLES

MV ACHILLES (sister ship AENEAS) was built for the Alfred Holt Co.

Maiden voyage was Dundee-Falmouth-Halifax (NS). It was Blue Funnel practice to carry out their official trial on the maiden voyage from Dundee. The local trial out of Dundee was to sort out any major problems if any.

Ships of the Alfred Holt Line ,"Holters", never returned alongside at the Caledon if the local trial was acceptable and the trials party was tendered ashore.[JR]

She answered an SOS from the Panamanian steamer NORLANDA reported sinking near the Azores 1/2/48. Achilles made 14.5 knots in very heavy weather but SOS cancelled 3.5 hours after issue. Transferred to the Glen line and renamed RADNORSHIRE and retransferred to the Blue Funnel line and renamed ASPHALION. Transferred to the Nederlandsche Stoomvart in 1966 and renamed POLYPHEMUS.

Transferred in 1972 to the Ocean Group. Sold to Gulf Shipping of Liverpool for $650,000 in 1973 and renamed GULF ANCHOR. Aground at Demman Mari and scrapped at Taiwan 1979.[1]

Built 1947   **Yard No** 430

Specifications
8295 Gross tons
450 x 62 x 35 feet

Machinery
Diesel 6800 BHP by Harland & Wolf
8 Cyls Dia 550mm Stroke 1600 combined
Opposed piston
15.5 knots

Complement
12 Passengers   70 Crew

ML SCHWEDAGA

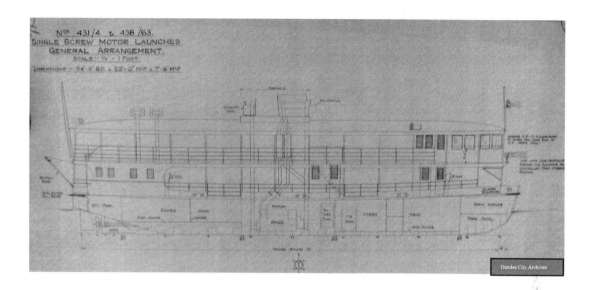

Motor Launch SCHWEDAGA was built for the Irrawady Flotilla Co. which operated in Burma.

There were 29 of these vessels built at this time i.e. Nos 431 to 434 and 438 to 463 and were to replace vessels scuttled by their owners on the Japanese invasion of Burma.[2] Rudyard Kipling was inspired by the old steam paddle boats to include the following lines in his poem "Mandalay":

"Come you back to Mandalay

Where the old Flotilla lay

Can't you hear the paddles chunkin'

From Rangoon to Mandalay"

The launches were prefabricated in sections and shipped to Rangoon. Their manufacture took place on any spare area available in the yard.

No photograph has been found of a completed vessel.

Built 1947	**Yard No** 431

Specifications
110 Gross tons
94 x 22 x 7 feet

Machinery
Diesel by Crossley

nd knots

Complement
nd Passengers nd Crew

95

MV ENGLAND

MV ENGLAND was built for the Currie Line of Leith. She was in collision in fog off Cape Villano 15/4/51 (with an unknown vessel believed Spanish) bound Genoa to London. Damage treated with cement boxes placed over holes in forepeak. Proceeded at 6kn until cement hardened. Several collisions on the Genoa to London route.

Sold to Greek owners Harikat in 1967 and renamed NIKOLAS KATSOULIS and renamed again MACO TRADER. Renamed FILIKOS in 1973 under ownership of Tenerife Shipping Company of Famgusta. Renamed GAMSOLO in 1973.

Detained at Nordkopping, after discharging fertilizer 3/74, by inspection authorities and certificate of seaworthiness withdrawn and also boycotted by the port workers federation.

She broke bail on 17/3/74. Several crew were in hospital with smoke inhalation from fires set to put some heat in the ship the boilers being out of action. She sailed with open hatches and unsecured derricks ignoring the coastguard hail. The customs officers attempted to board her but were unable to do so and shots were fired across her bow. She reached international waters but was tracked by radar and aircraft.

She had a Faroese master whose home town was Singapore. Renamed KETIGA she arrived at Rotterdam 22/3/74 and was arrested at the instigation of the Swedish firm who claimed 500 tons of fertilizer were damaged at Nordkopping. Port authorities lashed the wheel to the wheelhouse . The crew also instigated arrest for non payment of wages. Matters were cleared in a few days and she left Rotterdam on17/4/74.[1]

After several changes of name she went in 1978 as KUNTA to the breakers National Iron and Steel board of Singapore.[6]

Built 1947	**Yard No** 435

Specifications
2271 Gross tons
315 x 46 x 28 feet

Machinery
Diesel 2000 IHP by Kincaid of Greenock
4 Cyls Dia 630mm Stroke 1300mm
12 knots

Complement
0 Passengers   37 Crew

Continued opposite

The launch day was one of celebration and representatives of the owners and also local Dundee dignitaries would attend to view the launch and afterwards attend a reception in the Caledon Boardroom. The speech from the owners representative at the MV ENGLAND launch has survived, which is rare. It is reproduced here in full in order to convey the atmosphere of the occasion; clearly events of the day had been satisfactory. A stage payment cheque would have been paid to the Caledon after a successful launch. Mrs R F Scovell launched the ship.

Mr R F Scovell Proposing the health of the Builders.

"It seems to have become fashionable recently at launches for owners to complain about slow delivery and of the austerity materials which builders are compelled to use. Let me say immediately that we have no such complaints against the Caledon company.

SCOTLAND was delivered to us on 15th October and there was nothing austere about her. She is to our minds a first class vessel in every way and her performance since entering service has been highly satisfactory. The General manager and other high officials of the Shipping Federation, as well as Union Officials, have been highly complimentary regarding the accommodation both for officers and for ratings. It is true that SCOTLAND's delivery was held up for some weeks on account of the failure of sub-contractors to deliver the "blower". Not being a technical man the "blower" only conveyed to my mind an intricate organization run by the starting price bookmakers whereby bets are passed from the bookies' offices to the race course. I am sure some of you who are stupid enough to visit race meetings must have seen the "blower" in action the shape of busy little men in bowler hats rushing down the rails just before the "Off" knocking down amateur race-goers in their mad progress. Now I hardly expected that even under present day conditions a ship needed to have a bookmaker's aboard but on consulting our Superintendents I discovered that the "blower" was a well-nigh essential part of the main engines. It is to be hoped that the "blower" for the vessel just launched will arrive in due time and I am given to understand that it is now in transit from Switzerland.

There is something about a Caledon ship. All those which we have built to our account with the Caledon Company have proved highly satisfactory. HENGIST, KIRKLAND and RUTLAND were lost during the War years. We have however recently built LAPLAND, ICELAND and SCOTLAND with our friends here and we are highly satisfied and now ENGLAND is to join them, we hope and trust, during the Spring. We also own two older vessels by the Caledon Company in 1920 FINLAND and FORELAND. These ships are in such condition that we have not hesitated to spend large sums of money on them recently, in spite of the fact that they are now 27 years of age. This shows that Caledon ships are built to last.

In 1943 the Minister of War Transport sent me on a mission to Turkey to advise the Turkish Government as to how to increase the efficiency of their Mercantile Marine. I had with me an experienced Marine Superintendent and the late manager of the Mazagon Dockyard Co. of Bombay. On our arrival at Istanbul our enthusiasm was somewhat damped by the sight of the decrepit museum pieces whose efficiency we were to improve. Some of these ships however were of outstanding beauty with their fiddle bows in the superb setting of the Golden Horn. We soon discovered however that there were only three ships which, to our minds, were ideally suited for the Turkish coastal trade and these were named KONYA, CANAKKALE and somewhat curiously the ANAFARTA. On having recourse to Lloyds Register we found that the KONYA had been built as the PERTH in 1890 for the Dundee Perth and London Co. and that the CANAKKALE and ANNAFARTA were originally the LIZARD and SKERRYVORE built for the Clyde Shipping Co. in 1895 and 1898. I maintain that these ships are a wonderful advertisement for the Caledon Co. and their predecessors W B Thompson & Co.- and my only hope is that the ships they are building today will also be alive and kicking fifty years hence.

I give you the health of the Caledon Co."

Mrs Scovell
Launches
MV ENGLAND

Mr & Mrs
Scovell and Mr
Henry Main

MV STAR of ASSUAN

MV STAR of ASSUAN was built for the Alexandria Navigation Company.
Intended for the Alexandria –Mersey service with occasional trips Egypt to Bombay and the Med to East Canada. She was on fire at Marseilles on 28/12/59 after blazing cotton in a dockside warehouse spread to a forward hold. Hatch covers were burnt as the ship was cleared. At Montreal in 1960 picket lines of the Seafarers International Union were experienced in return for blacklisting of certain Western ships by Egypt. 37 passengers were aboard. Dockers disregarded pickets and unloaded the cargo of cotton, rice and olives. On 30/12/69 she was adrift in bad weather at Alexandria.
She was one of the first vessels to pass through the Suez canal in 1974 when it was reopened.[1]

Built 1947   **Yard No** 437

Specifications
5392 Gross tons
375 x 55 x 32 feet

Machinery
Diesel 2500 BHP Doxford type by Scotts
of Greenock 2 stroke opposed piston
4 Cyl Dia 560 Stroke comb 2160
13 knots

Complement
40 Passengers   58 Crew

SS CALEDONIAN MONARCH

SS CALEDONIAN MONARCH was built for the Monarch Shipping Co of Glasgow . Her first master was Captain H J Downie of Freuchie. She returned to Dundee with 9000 tons sugar in 1950. One of five vessels damaged at Beira 27/6/53 by fire after a leakage of petrol from a tanker. Sold to Great Eastern Shipping of Bombay 5/7/58 for £230,000 and renamed JAA DOOT. In 1966 she was sold to New York Greeks for £150,000 and renamed CENTRAL AMERICA. In 1968 she was owned by World Wide Maritime of Monrovia and renamed SAINT FRANCIS.

Afire in the South Sulu Sea on 11/11/68 en route Davao to the European Continent with 6750 tons of copra. Fire was raging in all holds and the ship sides were red hot.

The crew were taken off by a Phillipines Naval vessel and landed at Zambeonga.

A tug got two men aboard and towed the ship which was yawing badly.[1]

Delivered to Raeburn & Verel, Managers; Ran trials in Tay Estuary.

In 1968 owned by the Arendal Shipping Corporation Liberia; World Wide Maritime Co., Ltd., Liberia, Managers.

1968 Abandoned by crew in Sulu Sea after fire broke out on 7 November whilst on passage Davao to Europe. Sank whilst under tow of tug Uranus.[6]

Built 1947	**Yard No** 464

Specifications
 6979 Gross tons
 425 x 56 x 27 feet

Machinery
Steam triple expansion   2500 IHP by
Kincaid of Greenock
Cyls 24.5 39 70/48   HP 220 psi
10.5 knots

Complement
 0 Passengers   43 Crew

MV CLYTONEUS

Dundee City Archives

MV CLYTONEUS was built for Alfred Holt Ltd of Liverpool. Her first master was Peter Elder of Dundee. The ship was launched by Mrs Powrie wife of the Lord Provost of Dundee. Lord Provost Powrie and his wife cruised the maiden voyage Dundee to the Clyde. In collision in the Thames on 23/1/64 with MV DOMBURGH.

Sold to Taiwan breakers in 1972. (Captain Elder became a nautical advisor to the Blue Funnel line retiring in 1963 and died at Birkenhead in August 1976).[1]

Transferred to the Elder Dempster line in 1971.[6]

Built 1948   **Yard No** 465

Specifications
 8213 Gross tons
 450 x 62 x 35 feet

Machinery
Diesel 6800 BHP (B&W type) by Kincaid
of Greenock
8 Cyl Dia 550 mm Stroke 1600mm Comb.
opposed piston 2 stroke
15 knots

Complement
32 Passengers   73 Crew

SS CITY of PERTH

SS CITY of PERTH was built for Ellerman Lines. She was the first City liner built at Dundee being one of 10 ordered simultaneously. She suffered superficial damage on 3/2/50 when maneuvering at Calcutta alongside CITY of OXFORD. Her superstructure was badly damaged by a falling crane at Dunkirk on 7/3/55.

The first cargo of linseed oil was discharged at Dundee in March 1955.

She was chartered in April 1958 for a 7000 ton part cargo of coal from Hampton roads to Chiba Japan. She suffered several collisions including sinking the Dutch MV PINTA off New Jersey on 7/5/63. She picked up 11 survivors before putting back to Hoboken for repairs. Sold in Greece to Astro Esperante Cie Navigation of Panama in November 1967 but wrecked at Great Pass Alexandria On 3/1/68 on maiden voyage from Rotterdam under the new owners. She was deeply laden to 29 feet draught and took a 12 degree list with the holds and engineroom flooded, Abandoned 5/1/68.[1]

Trial Trip 1949 on passage Dundee to Glasgow.

1967 Astro Aspirante Cia Nav.S.A. of Piraeus; Renamed ELENIF; Price reported to be over £165,000.

1968 Struck a Wreck at Alexandria; beached but broke in two in heavy seas; abandoned and stripped where she lay.[6]

Built 1948   **Yard No** 466

Specifications
 7546 Gross tons
 450 x 61 x 33 feet

Machinery
Steam turbine   7200 SHP by Parsons
3 stage single reduction gearbox
HP 275 psi
15 knots

Complement
12 Passengers   87 Crew

SS WOODLAND

Dundee City Archives

SS WOODLAND was built for the Currie Line. Sister ship PINELAND was also built at this time. On 12/4/51 her cargo of sugar (rail) cars broke loose in a gale 150miles west of Lands End and she put back to Falmouth. Two chassis were lost overboard due to heavy rolling and seven others shifted. Resumed her voyage Antwerp to San Domingo on April 17th. Sold to the Union Steamship Co. of New Zealand in 1954 for £210,000 and renamed KAPONGA. Sold to Heng Fung of Hong Kong and renamed NAM FENG. In August 1961 took logs from Mount Maunganui to Tokyo.

Sold to Phillipines owners Leecho SS Co of the Pescadores Group of Taiwan for £40,000 in 1963. Abandoned by crew of 33 when she took a 30 degree list bound Sedacan to Kochsiung with a cargo of logs. The after part was awash and the deck cargo was washing away and cracks were evident in No 3 hold.[1]

Wrecked off Taiwan in 1967 when she grounded on a small island South of Pescadores and became total loss.[6]

Built 1948	**Yard No** 468

Specifications
 2758 Gross tons
 300 x 46 x 23 feet

Machinery
Steam triple expansion   1700 IHP by
Kincaid of Greenock
Cyls 19 31 55/36   HP 220 psi
12 knots

Complement
2 Passengers 33 Crew

MV WANSTEAD

MV WANSTEAD was built for the Watts Watts Shipping Co of London. Sister ships WENDOVER and WOODFORD were also built at this time. Managing Director Mr G Parker lead the launch party.

These were the first of a new class of liners of revolutionary design for the Canada–Continent trade with a service speed of 15knots and consuming 18 tons of diesel fuel per day. Their new cost (to the owners) was £610,00 each. During early service she achieved an average of 14.72 knots on 16.7 tons fuel/day. Grounded near Quebec 14/11/1949 on maiden voyage from London to Montreal in ballast but refloated without assistance. Shell plates were set up between Nos 1&2 hold double bottoms and there were numerous leaky rivets. Temporary repairs were made at Montreal by fitting cement boxes. On 17/6/50 she was in collision the Dutch MV ALDABI at Flushing roads en route Montreal to Amsterdam. Proceeded with damage to Port side amidships and drydocked at Amsterdam. Time chartered to the Port Line in 1957 and renamed PORT WANSTEAD. On 23/2/60 in collision with and holed Russian ship GRIJBEJDOY off Walsanden on the Scheldt . Renamed WANSTEAD in 1960 and laid up at Barrow in 1962. Time chartered to the Lamport & Holt line and renamed ROEBURN. Renamed WENLUI on transfer to Far East service on 10 year bareboat charter to China Navigation Co. In 1969 on fire at Yokohama on Nov 5 bound Kobe to Melbourne. Fire extinguished with CO2. She was aquired by the China Navigation Co. in 1969. At Melbourne in February 1971 officers were attacked while watching TV by the Chinese crew resulting in 26 Chinese arrested but released the following day. One officer jumped overboard and 2 Chinese were injured. Captain Ronald Pook and the Second Engineer Robert Lansford were relieved after Chinese protests. The ship had been "blacked" by the dockers. She was sold to Maldive Shipping of Male' in 1975, renamed MALDIVE EXPLORER and ultimately scrapped at Gadani Beach Karachi in 1978.[1]

Built 1949	**Yard No** 469

Specifications
 5664 Gross tons
 440 x 64 x 43 feet

Machinery
Diesel 5500 BHP by Scott (Doxford) of Greenock.
5 Cyl 670mm Stroke 2320mm Comb.
Opposed piston 2 stroke

15 knots
Complement
0 Passengers 48 Crew

MV BELLEROPHON

MV BELLEROPHON was built for Alfred Holt Ltd. Transferred to the Glen & Shire Lines in 1957 and renamed CARDIGANSHIRE later retransferred to Blue Funnel renamed BELLEROPHON. In February 1974 loaded three 84 ton transformers at Liverpool for Ulsan Korea. In October 1975 chartered for 10-14 days by Haworth productions for film making at Dartmouth. The film story was about men having to choose between rival loves i.e. girl friends and the sea. The ship name was shortened to BELL and flew the US flag for filming. She was sold in 1976 to OPPP Navigation lines of Jeddah Saudi Arabia for $950,000 and renamed OBHAR. In collision NW of Port Said on 18/4/78 with unknown vessel carrying containers and under tow showing no lights. OBHAR stopped to check damage and safety of crew but the other vessel did not stop. OBHAR proceeded to Antwerp. Scrapped at Gadani Beach Karachi 1978.[1]
1978 Arrived at Gadani Beach , Karachi, for breaking up.

1978 beached for Modern Commercial Corporation.[6]

Built 1950   **Yard No** 473

Specifications
 7706 Gross tons
 450 x 62 x 35 feet

Machinery
Diesel 6800 BHP by Kincaid of Greenock
7 Cyls Dia 750mm Stroke 2000mm comb.
15 knots

Complement
12 Passengers   74 Crew

SS EDDY BEACH

SS EDDY BEACH (Tanker, Fleet oiler) was built for HM Admiralty Naval Stores Dept. Sister ship EDDY BAY was also built about this time. At Coronation review Spithead 15/6/53. Laid up at Devonport 1962 and for sale 1963. Sold to Greek Tankshipping Co Ltd Piraeus in 1964 and renamed MYKINAI. Sold in 1972 to the Greek Atlantic Fishing Co Ltd. In 1974 owned by Mediterranean Austral SA of Buenos Aires (Stern trawling factory ship).

On 7/10/74 she suffered an engineroom explosion at Mar del Plata with sabotage suspected. The afterpart sunk and rested on the bottom. On 8/7/75 she was struck by the trawler MELINOI at Mar del Plata, both being damaged. Owners intended to repair her but nothing could be done until completion of judicial enquiry into bomb explosion. In 1979 she sank at her moorings.[1]

Royal Fleet Auxiliary. Pennant No. A132.[6]

Built 1951   **Yard No** 474

Specifications
 2157 Gross tons
 425 x 56 x 38 feet

Machinery
Steam triple expansion   1750 IHP
By Lobnitz of Renfrew
Cyls 16 27.5 43.5/21   HP 240 psi
12 knots

Complement
27 Passengers   31Crew

MV AIDA

Dundee City Archives

MV AIDA was built for Raderi A/B Wallenco. Sister ship SUNNAS built about the same time (pictured). She lost her starboard anchor and 30 fathoms of cable at Bitter lakes 17/9/51 bound Port de Boue to Massawah. Badly ashore at Marmora Island, Sea of Marmora 7/11/53 with part cargo of 3281 tons of benzene and1405 tons of kerosene bound Istanbul to Izmir. Following an SOS the salvage steamer KILYOS was in attendance with AIDA close to cliffs and badly damaged forward but her engine room intact. In the heavy weather the salvage steamers were sheltering and part of her crew was transferred to the motor vessel FERNEBA and landed at Istanbul. In getting free AIDA had to jettison 1717 tons of benzene and 264 tons of kerosene. She proceeded to Spezia 23/11/53 accompanied by IMRAZ and HERAKLES took over outside the Dardanelles. Repairs were carried out at Marseilles.

She was badly damaged in collision with tanker TOBIAS U BORTHEN in the Musi River, Indonesia April 1962 sustaining a huge hole in the bows. Repaired in 16 days at Kowloon, Hong Kong with 145 tons of steel required. Sold in 1964 to Cia Financiere Malaya S.A. Panama for £150,000 and renamed ARGO NOVIS managed by Leonia Shipping Corp. Inc. Piraeus. Sold to Taiwan breakers 1969 arriving at Kaohsiung on 21st March.[1]

MV SUNNAAS was aground on a sandbank in Chesapeake bay 3-5/11/59 bound Curacao – Baltimore with oil. She was sold to Bermuda flag buyers in 1962 for £75,000 and converted at Verolmer yard Rotterdam as an offshore workshop for service in oil drilling areas.

A 300 ton crane was fitted. New owners Global Offshore Contractors Ltd.

Renamed GLOBAL ADVENTURER for Global Offshore Structures Ltd and to be used for sinking oil drills in deep water. Managed by Nederlands Vicet Tankveert Maets SV Willemstad. In January 1965 at Rotterdam from German Bight.

She crushed the tug MASTERMAN on 6/2/66 against the drilling rig Conoco No 1 which was being sunk in the Humber. The crew was picked up and the tug was released and reached port. While in the Humber "stepped" new dockgates at Immingham with its heavy derrick. Transferred to Brown and Root Co SA Panama.

Under refit at Table Bay for 6 weeks in 1969 for use in undersea oil exploration off Angola. Sold to Selco (Singapore) Ltd Sept 1975 for demolition in Taiwan.

Built 1951	**Yard No** 475

Specifications
9488 Gross tons
470 x 64 x 35 feet
Machinery
Diesel 4500 BHP by Vickers Armstrong of Barrow (Doxford)
4 Cyl Dia 670 mm Stroke 2320mm
Comb.
Opposed piston 2 stroke
12.5 Knots

Complement
0 Passengers 45 Crew

MV SANDA

Dundee City Archives

MV SANDA was built for the Clyde Shipping Co of Glasgow. Sister ship PLADDA was also built at this time. Had engine trouble in the Pentland Firth 1/3/50 on maiden voyage to the Clyde. Drifted North west with the tide until the crew made emergency repairs. Anchored at Scrabster and repairs effected. Resumed passage 2/3/50. Slight damage after collision with MV SAPPHIRE at Dublin 13/9/50. Two other minor collisions. Transferred in December 1959 to the Belfast to London run when the Glasgow to Cork service was suspended after 103 years. Sold for £52,500 to Guan Guan Shipping Co of Singapore in1963 and renamed SUMUI MAS. Adrift in the Mediterranean with main engine breakdown bound Glasgow to Singapore. Towed to Alexandria by tug MISSISSIPI 11/9/63. Sold in 1964 to Transport Maritimes San SA Panama and renamed ZOLA. Sold to Cia de Nav. Santos SA, Panama and renamed BONNY. Name changed several times 1965-1969 and finally as GOLDEN WELL of Singapore she stranded in 1969 and was a total loss.[1]

Built 1949	Yard No 476

Specifications
 853 Gross tons
 200 x 38 x 15 feet

Machinery
Diesel 1190 BHP by Polar Atlas of
Glasgow
7 Cyl 340mm dia Stroke 570 mm
2 stroke single acting
12 knots

Complement
0 Passengers   19 Crew

TSMV St NINIAN

Dundee City Archives

TSMV St NINIAN was built for The North of Scotland Steamship Co for Orkney and Shetland service to Aberdeen and Leith.

She saved the crew of four from the fishing vessel WHYTE JOHN abandoned on fire off Montrose 2/10/50. Slightly damaged alongside quay at Aberdeen 14/5/57 when arrester wires broke after launch of MV SUGAR PRODUCER ; later she struck quay wall and rebounded against bridge of St Ninian.

For 20 years she left Leith Monday 9pm, Aberdeen Tuesday 5pm arriving Kirkwall Wednesday morning, Lerwick Wednesday afternoon. Left Lerwick Thursday morning, Kirkwall Friday morning arriving Aberdeen Saturday morning and Leith Saturday evening.

In February 1971 she was withdrawn from the Leith–Aberdeen-Kirkwall-Lerwick run and sold to Atlantique Cruises of Nova Scotia crossing from Aberdeen to Halifax in 9 days. In service from North Sydney to St Pierre and Miquelon after a few days of arrival with same name and some crew retained. In 1972 she was refitted for dancing, cabaret, and with a gaming room and 3 bars and lounges including a duty free store for bonded goods. In April she set off on an angler's expedition to St Albans Newfoundland, comparable to the Norwegian Fiords. Helicopters were included to whisk passengers inland to see herds of caribou and moose in uninhabitable terrain.

In 1975 described in Lloyds register as passenger ferry/livestockcarrier/reefer.

Sold to Ecuador owners in 1976 and lying at Halifax Newfoundland. Renamed BUCCANEER the owners being the Galapagos Tourist Corporation, Guayaquil and listed as accommodating 90 berth passengers rather than 390.

In 1978 renamed as BUCCNERA. Same owners.[1]

Sold in 1991 to Akeiras Del Wcuador S.A. Demolition commenced at Guayaquil, Ecuador during 1991[6]

Built 1950   **Yard No** 478

Specifications
 2242 Gross tons
 260 x 46 x 18 feet

Machinery
 Diesel 2620 BHP twin by Polar Atlas of
 Glasgow 2 stroke SA
 2 x 8 Cyl Dia 340mm Stroke 570mm

 14 knots
 Complement
 284 Passengers   26 Crew

108

TSMV KIMANIS

TSMV KIMANIS was built for the Straits Steamship Co. for the Singapore-Miri-Labuan-Jesseltan-Kudat Sendokan-Tawau service with 40 1st class, 24 2nd and 472 deck passengers. She was in collision at Singapore with MV BONNY (Caledon 1949) and slightly damaged. [1]

Built 1951	Yard No 481

Specifications
 3189 Gross tons
 285 x 51 x 29 feet

Machinery
Diesel (twin) 2560 BHP by British Polar
of Glasgow
2 x 8 Cyl Dia 340mm stroke 570mm
2 stroke SA
14 knots

Complement
514 Passengers   84 Crew

MV TABOR

MV TABOR was built for the Moss Hutchison Line of Liverpool. She was launched not showing a name during a painter's strike. Black listed in September 1955 by Egypt for allegedly carrying cargo for Israel. A fire in a store room, while at Monklands Wharf Glasgow on 25/12/58, was extinguished within a half hour. Had arrived from Cyprus with 1773 tons of cargo including 23,210 cases of oranges. On 12/1/61 she suffered an engine breakdown off Pantallaria bound Liverpool to Tel Aviv and was towed to Malta by destroyer HMS JUTLAND.
Sold in 1975 to Greek owners Apolloniave Shipping Co of Piraeus and renamed KATIA. En route Aegean to Constanze she stranded in the Bosphorus after striking a jetty in fog at Sariver on the European shore while under control of the pilot. Stranded for 4.5 hours she was refloated, examined and proceeded.[1]

1971 P.& O General Cargo Division appointed managers
1982 Kate Shipping Co.,Ltd., Malta; renamed KATE
Resold to Steel Industrials Kerala Ltd, India for demolition; Arrived at Beypore, Kerala State, India for demolition.[6]

Built 1951	**Yard No** 482

Specifications
 3694 Gross tons
 360 x 55 x 23 feet

Machinery
4450 BHP by Hawthorn Leslie (Doxford)
4 cyl 670mm Dia 2320mm Stroke Comb.
2 stroke opposed piston
12 knots

Complement
4 Passengers   45 Crew

SS BILLITON

SS BILLITON was built for MV Stoomvart of the Netherlands.
16 knots 10,800 dw. Engines were allocated to the Netherlands after WW2 and the hull was built to suit them. She broke down on 17/4/53 due to the thrust block running hot 7.5 hours after leaving San Francisco for Los Angeles and Laurenco Marques. She anchored in Half Moon Bay from where she was towed back to San Francisco by two tugs on 20/4/53. On 28/11/64 bound from New Orleans to Khorramshahr, Iran she put back to Beaumont damaged after collision with an oil barge.
From 2-5 May/64 she was on fire in two holds at Houston en route Khorramshahr to New York resulting in jute, timber and plastic flowers damaged and pineapple and dessicated coconut affected. Purchased by Mercury Sea Inc of Hong Kong, Panama registration and renamed MERCURY SEA. Sold to breakers at Kaohsiung, Taiwan 1974.[1]

Built   1950   **Yard No** 483

Specifications
 7444 Gross tons
 465 x 66 x 42 feet

Machinery
Steam turbine 9350 SHP @ 88RPM, cross cpd double reduction gearbox, by General Electric of USA.
16 knots

Complement
12 Passengers   71 Crew

FERRY SCOTSCRAIG

Ferry MV SCOTSCRAIG was built for Dundee Harbour trust for the Dundee to Newport ferry crossing. Launched by Mrs F J D Buist. Holed on 14/2/53 alongside Craig pier by "sitting" on a rock at low water; she was drydocked and back in service in 3 days.

She was withdrawn when the Tay Road Bridge opened on August 18 1966 and laid up in Victoria Dock until February 1968.

In 1968 she was sold to Pounds Shipowners and Shipbrokers Ltd of Portsmouth (£15,000 with ABERCRAIG) and sold on to Salvatore Bezzina of Malta. Reported in 1975 to be under conversion at Malta for oil exploration.. Transferred from Dundee to Malta register in 1977.[1]

In 1980 was used as a prop in making of film "Popeye" at Anchor Bay on the North side of the Island of Malta. Later towed out to sea and scuttled.[6]

Built 1951   **Yard No** 484

Specifications
462 Gross tons
168 x 36 x 8 feet

Machinery
Diesel twin 740 BHP total by English Electric 2 x 6 Cyl 10" bore 12" stroke
10 knots

SS NESTOR

SS NESTOR was built for the Alfred Holt shipping line. Sister ship NELIUS was built about the same time. She had engine trouble after leaving Liverpool for Brisbane on her maiden voyage 28/10/52 and anchored in Moelfre Roads returning to Liverpool on October 30th resuming on Oct 31. Transferred to Glen line in 1968 renamed GLENAFFRIC. Transferred to Blue Funnel line in1970 renamed ORESTES.
Sold to Kimon Cie Nav SA of Panama (Aegis group) in 1971and renamed AEGIS DIGNITY. Sold to Adelais Maritime Co Famagusta in 1972. In 1973, bound Alexandria to Gdansk there were "serious" differences between 12 Ghanain crew members and senior officers. The 12 were landed at Valletta on August 13th.
Sold for demolition at Whampoa (China) in 1974.[1]

SS NELEUS was built for A.Holt & Co., Managers Liverpool.
1971 Akamas Shipping Co., Cyprus.
1974 Alicarnassos Shipping Co., Cyprus; Re named AEGIS TRUST.
1974 Left Nigata,Japan for demolition at Shanghai.[6]

Built 1952		**Yard No** 485

Specifications
7802 Gross tons
453 x 64 x 35 feet

Machinery
Steam turbine 8000 SHP (Pametrada design) by Metrovick of Trafford Park Cross compound with double reduction gearbox.   HP 600psi 950F
nd knots

Complement
0 Passengers   75 Crew

MV BARON KILMARNOCK

MV BARON KILMARNOCK, tanker, was built for H Hogarth shipping Co.

This was the largest ship built on the Scottish East coast at the time. 11810 tons gross. Aground at Fredrickstadt 23/4/56, enroute Trinidad to Parsgrunn, resulting in propeller damage. Sold Det Bergenske Demps 1957 for £1.5 million including time charter of 20/6/57 expiring March 1958, renamed SPICA. Sold to Formosa owners for £180,000 Sept 1966. renamed EASTLAND TRADER. Under conversion at Hong Kong to bulk carrier. Had changed hands at Hong Kong to far East buyer. Chartered to Japan for 3 years for Pacific trade. Owners San Antonio SS Co Panama.

Renamed LAVENDER in1973 under new owners Lavender Corp. Panama.

Renamed SOUTHMONT in 1977 owners Island Enterprises (Private) Ltd Singapore.

Renamed BLOOMFIELD in 1977 same owners, suffered engine failure near Prates Reef 16/4/78 and towed to Hong Kong.

Scrapped at Kaohsiung 1979.[1]

Built   1952   **Yard No** 487

Specifications
 11,810 Gross tons
 515 x 71 x 39 feet

Machinery
 Diesel 6950 BHP by Kincaid of Greenock
 6 Cyls Dia 750mm Stroke 2000mm
 14 knots

Complement
 0 Passengers   31+ Crew

MV WOKINGHAM

Dundee City Archives

MV WOKINGHAM was built for the Watts Watts Shipping company. (Sister ship WOOLWICH (pictured) was built about the same time.) Damaged in collision with Portuguese SS SETE CIDEDAS in lower Elbe 4/7/58/ bound Baltimore-Szezecin. On fire in No3 hold and engineroom at Shanghai 4/7/60 but extinguished the same day. Had arrived from Lethakia. Towed to Hong Kong for repairs 16/8/60. Laid up at Barrow Sept 1962 till early 1963 along with WINDSOR (built Glasgow). The pair sold for £385,000. Wokingham became JAG KRANTI. She sold for £214,000 in 1967 to Giannes Nav Co Cyprus and renamed CASTRALIA. She collided with the Mackinac bridge between Detroit and Chicago 2/6/68 in fog with 40 bow plates damaged plus internals. Repaired at Chicago. Aground in the Welland canal 23/7/68 sustaining bottom damage. Sold to Gulf Shipping of Karachi in 1975 for $405,000 renamed UNITED SUCCESS. Sold to a Japanese trading Co. in 1977 and broken up 1977.

MV WOOLWICH 1955 #491 Towed back to the Mersey on 13/6/57 with main engine failure when bound Manchester to USA. Sold to the Bulgarian Mercantile fleet for £535,000 in 1962 and renamed LUBEN KARAVELOV . Deal was for 10% down and remainder over 4 years. Scrapped in 1976 in Yugoslavia.)[1]

MV WOOLWICH 1962 Sold for £535,000 to Navigation Maritime Bulgare; Renamed LUBEN KARAVELOV. Port of Registry Varna.[6]

Built 1953   **Yard No** 488

Specifications
7659 Gross tons
435 x 58 x 38 feet

Machinery
Diesel 4400BHP (Doxford) by Vickers of
Barrow 4 Cyls
Dia 670mm Stroke 2320mm comb

14 knots

Complement
0 Passengers 41 Crew

MV TEMPLEHALL

MV TEMPLEHALL was built for the Temple Steamship Company of London. Shown on the left above alongside King George V wharf in Dundee with the MV CITY OF DUNDEE lying immediately to the East. All three ships in this early 1960's scene are Caledon built.[DM]

Chartered to the Brocklebank line for India round trip 1957. Struck by P&O liner SHILLONG on 7/10/57 in Royal Albert Dock London with a lifeboat smashed and other damage totalling £15,000. SHILLONG sunk in collision a fortnight later. Engaged for four months carrying troops and equipment during the Suez emergency 1956-7. Damaged in collision with Indonesian ship SS HAILONE at Belawan 17/10/61 in confusion following explosion on a petrol-laden barge.

Cargo shifted during a gale 20/1/65 en route Cardiff-Basrah and hove to 140 miles SW of Lands End. Sold in 1969 to Greek owners of Piraeus for £322,500 and renamed PANTELIS. Sold to Telemon maritime SA , Greece for $800,000 in 1977 renamed TELEMON. Collided July 1978 with Greek ship MV PALMYRA and British MV PRISEUS both anchored off Lagos. Cause was engine failure in TELEMON and there was resulting water damage to the cargo of cement.[1]

In 1981 while on voyage from San Pedro, Ivory Coast to Thessaloniki with cargo of logs she sprang a leak; beached at Arrecife, Lanzarote. Broke in two; broken up as she lies.[6]

Built 1954   **Yard No** 489

Specifications
 8003 Gross tons
 425 x 58 x 38 feet

Machinery
Diesel 3300 BHP (Doxford) by Vickers of Barrow
4 Cyls Dia 600mm Stroke 2320mm

11.5 knots

Complement
0 Passengers   48 Crew

MV EUMAEUS

MV EUMAEUS was built for the Alfred Holt Shipping line of Liverpool.
On fire SW of Colombo en route Yokohama to Liverpool with tarpaulins and hatch covers alight on No.6 hold.
Extinguished with hoses.
In June 1958 she was commandeered by the Ceylon Government to take Tamil refugees to other parts of the Island during racial disturbances. Sold to Taiwan breakers in 1978.[1]
1962 Transferred to N.S.M. renamed OCEAAN; Amsterdam.

1978 Arrived at Kaohsiung,Taiwan for breaking up by Hai Kwang.[6]

Built   1953   **Yard No** 490

Specifications
7869 Gross tons
453 x 62 x 35 feet

Machinery
Diesel 7000 BHP by Harland & Wolff of
Belfast 7 Cyl Dia 750mm Stroke 2000mm
comb.(Opposed piston type)

nd knots

Complement
12 Passengers   73 Crew

SS EDDYREEF

Dundee City Archives

SS EDDYREEF , fleet oil tanker, was built for the British Admiralty. (Sister ship EDDYCOVE was built about the same time.) Engineroom flooded because of valve being accidentally left open at Harwich February 1955. She was beached and pumped out and towed on March 8 to Immingham for repairs. She was aground on a landspit off Bute on 4/7/55 and was refloated by two naval tugs and berthed alongside HMS ADAMANT.
Sold to Bergen shipbreakers at Antwerp in 1964.[1]
Royal Fleet Auxiliary Pennant No. A262.
Laid up in 1962 with surveys overdue. 1964 sold for scrap.[6]

Built 1953	**Yard No** 492

Specifications
2219 Gross tons
270 x 44 x 18 feet

Machinery
Steam Triple exp. 1750 IHP by Lobnitz of
Renfrew Cyls 16 27.5 43.5/31 HP 240psi

12 knots

Complement
 27 Passengers   41Crew

MV SWIFTPOOL

MV SWIFTPOOL was built for the Sir R Ropner shipping Co of West Hartlepool.

Intended for the London – Miami–Gulf liner service. Passenger fares £90 single £200 round voyage. Damaged when fitting out at Caledon Boilershop following collision with tanker SECOMET berthing at King George Wharf 29/5/1954. On 29/6/1954 she developed engine trouble while manoeuvering to enter Maimi on her maiden voyage. Drifted north, anchored and arrived the following day. At the time she was the beamiest ship to enter the Manchester ship canal at 63ft 7inches. The liner service was withdrawn in June 1956 and she was switched to tramp trades (i.e.took cargo from place to place anywhere where work could be found). Chartered by the Strick line in 1957 rated at 16 knots on 26 tons of diesel/day. Laid up briefly at Hull in 1958. Laid up at Middlesborough for 8 months in 1962. Sold to British India Steam Navigation Co. while on time charter for the West Africa trade; renamed CHAKLA.

Sold in 1972 to Guan Guan Shipping (Private) Ltd of Singapore and renamed GOLDEN BEAR. Scrapped in 1975 at Yun Shen Steel and Ironworks Taiwan.[1]

Built 1954   **Yard No** 494

Specifications
6725 Gross tons
450 x 63x 41 feet

Machinery
Diesel 8000 BHP opposed piston by Alex
Stephen of Glasgow
6 Cyls 725mm Dia 2250mm stroke comb.

16 knots

Complement
 14 Passengers   44 Crew

SS BARON GLENCONNER

SS BARON GLENCONNER was built for H Hogarth (Kelvin Shipping Co).
She was disabled with boiler trouble 29.4N 14.4E on June 26 1962 en route Rotterdam-Beira (Clan Line charter). Towed to Las Palmas by tug FORTUNATE June 28-9 sailing on July 18. Sold in 1963 to Ilissus Marine Corporation of Monrovia for £145,000 and renamed ZITA. Engine breakdown 27N 76W bound Boca Grande to Liverpool and towed from Freeport, Bahamas, to the UK.
Sold for £215,000 in 1965 to Taiwan International Line Ltd of Keelung Formosa. And renamed KUO YANG. Grounded at Muicien on 7/5/67 from San Francisco. 100 tons of steel needed for repairs. Sold in 1968 to the Hai Seng Co. of Keelung Formosa and renamed CONVOY PIONEER. Sold in 1969 to the Amerworld Nav. Co. of Monrovia renamed AMWORLD. Anchored 360 miles short of Kuwait with engine trouble in July 1971 when bound Karachi to Kuwait with cement. Failure was caused by a broken main engine medium pressure cylinder cover. Towed to Kuwait 29/7 by Smit tug BARENTS ZEE. Scrapped at Kaohsiung in 1973 by Tung Ho Steel Enterprise Co.[1]

Built 1955	**Yard No** 495

Specifications
5468 Gross tons
450 x 38 x 57 feet

Machinery
Steam 3000 BHP triple exp. With Bauer
Wach exhaust turbine by J G Kincaid of
Greenock Cyls 24.5 41 68/48

nd knots

Complement
0 Passengers 42 Crew

MV STORAAS

Dundee City Archives

MV STORAAS, tanker, was built for Iver Bugge shipping Co of Larvik Norway.

This was the largest ship built at the Caledon and the largest vessel built on the Scottish East Coast. The slip at Caledon yard was extended specially into the "market" an area beneath the clock where day hire was once the practice. In collision in the Hudson river with the American tanker GULFMOON but with no damage. Grounded entering Dublin 29/12/57 ; went astern and refloated without damage berthing at Ocean pier. On 1/4/66 she was aground laden off Puerta Cortez without damage.

Renamed SAGA SCOUT in 1967 under same owners. Sold in 1969 to Cia de Nav. Buena S.A. of Panama and renamed KINGSLAND TRADER (Liberian Flag).

Sold to Escudo Shipping Corporation of Liberia in 1969.

In August 1971 she was in trouble at Baltimore where the Filipino master left the ship under police guard after a dispute with the Chinese crew over food. The master was alleged to have struck the chief steward with the butt of a shotgun because he feared assault. The crew gave no trouble as master left. On the previous day police went to the vessel at anchor to remove two officers who were charged with illegal entry to the USA and deported. Liberian Consulate said that the vessel's registration papers were removed because of defective wiring on the ship. Repairs were needed to make her safe. The Master flew to Manila and a replacement took over. The crew complained that they had been forced to subsist on a diet of rice and under the new master they received fresh meat and vegetables. The Chinese mate said that the trouble was due to the master not being able to speak Chinese.

In 1971she was transferred to the Panama flag. Scrapped at Kaohsiung 1972.[1]

Sir R.Ropner & Co., Managers; For U.K. Mexico Service.[6]

Built 1954	**Yard No** 497

Specifications
12075 Gross tons
530 x 72 x 39 feet

Machinery
Diesel 8000 BHP opposed piston 2 stroke
by Harland & Wolff of Belfast
7 Cyl   Dia 750mm Stroke 2000mm comb.

14 knots

Complement
0 Passengers   52 Crew

121

SS THESEUS

Dundee City Archives

SS THESEUS was built for the Ocean Steamship Co (Alfred Holt). She grounded off Dunkirk Mar 19 1966 en route Brisbane to the Continent; no apparent damage. Renamed AEGIS MYTH in 1971 when sold to New Kimon SA (Aegis Group) of Panama for £200,000. Chartered to Volte Lines for West African service. Owners Alkividis shipping SA Panama. Registered Famagusta.

Renamed AEGIS CARE in 1972 under ownership of Syracuse Shipping Co Ltd Famagusta. Sold to breakers at Shanghai 1974.[1]

Built 1955   **Yard No** 498

Specifications
7804 Gross tons
453 x 64 x 35 feet

Machinery
Steam turbine 8000 SHP Cross cpd double
reduction gearbox by Metro-Vickers of
Manchester.   HP 625 psi

16 knots

Complement
0 Passengers   74 Crew

MV PERLIS

MV PERLIS was built for the Straits steamship Co of Singapore. In 1970 her owners were Sherikat Perkalopen Kpis San Berkad (Manfield & Co) Lebuan, Brunei.[1]
Straits Steamship Co.,Ltd., East Indian Archipelago Service; Company later became Straits Shipping Pte. Ltd., Singapore. Port of Register Singapore; Manfield & Co. Ltd., Managers.
1984 Sold to National Shipbreakers Pte. Ltd., Singapore. Demolition began at Singapore.[6]

Built 1954   **Yard No** 499

Specifications
1414 Gross tons
195 x 40 x 19 feet

Machinery
Diesel 1580 BHP 4 stroke geared by
Ruston & Hornsby of Lincoln.
8-Cyls 10.25" Dia 14.5" Stroke

9.5 knots

Complement
6 +83 Passengers   53 Crew

MV City of Winnipeg

MV CITY OF WINNIPEG was built for Ellerman Lines. She suffered a small fire in the focsle at Mombasa 25/2/60. After being damaged by ice off Cape Breton in April 1962 she arrived at Corner Brook.

In 1966 she broke from her mooring buoy during heavy weather ay Yokohama on 25/11/66 and collided with COHSHU MARU (4906 t); both slightly damaged.

In 1968 she was sold to the Ben Line under Far East services and renamed BENEDIN. Disabled with engine trouble, 3N 10.52 W   2/10/69 en route Hamburg to Manila, she was taken in tow by BENRINNES on Oct3. She Arrived at Monrovia 4/10/69 weather good. Cause was fractured oil pump shaft.

Renamed CITY of DELHI in 1971 on transfer to Ellerman line. Renamed FEXL GLORY in 1976 under ownership of Beaumaris Shipping Inc of Liberia. Fully loaded for Nagoya she was damaged in collision with MV JOY ARTI at Sitra anchorage Bahrain 1/11/76. Hull damage sustained.[1]

Completed for the Hall Line as Managers; Ran Trials at Skelmorlie.
1980 Arrived at Chittagong for breaking up.[6]

Built 1956   **Yard No** 500

Specifications
5468 Gross tons
 470 x 65 x 42 feet

Machinery
8000 BHP (Doxford type) by Wallsend
Slipway & Engineering Co
6 Cyl Dia 750mm   2500mm stroke.

16 knots

Complement
0 Passengers   86 Crew

MV DIOMED

Dundee City Archives

MV DIOMED was built for Alfred Holt (China Mutual Shipping Co) and was the cadet training ship for the Alfred Holt company carrying 11 on first voyage and 11 on second. This was Holt's 24th identical vessel, externally, since 1947. Early vessels required 69 feet long engine room and developed 6800 shp. DIOMED had a 63 feet long engine room and developed 8500 shp.

In 1957 she made her second voyage to the Far East via Panama in view of the Suez Canal closure.

Any profit made by the ship being manned by cadets rather than seamen was paid into the CALCHAS Fund named after a previous cadet ship. This funded seamen wishing to qualify as second mates and also marine charities. The cadet accommodation was given over to crew after a new training hostel, AULIS, opened in Liverpool.

She was in collision with and sank the Japanese salvage steamer AKI MARU at Nagoya 19/12/63. The Japanese master drowned but 6 others were saved. DIOMED was undamaged.

She was transferred to the Glen Line in1970 and renamed GLENBEG. On fire in No3 hold in October 1970 at the Royal Docks, London. The cargo was palm oil, fibre, tea and plywood for Hamburg and Rotterdam; 6 fire appliances, 100 firemen and a fire float attended. Thousands of cubic feet of foam were applied to the fire which was centred deep down in the plywood. No apparent structural damage but 170 tons tea and 70 bales of plywood were damaged. She transferred to Blue Funnel in 1972 and was renamed DIOMED.

Sold to Far eastern owners in 1973 and renamed KAISING she was managed by the Ocean Tramping Co Ltd of Mogadishu. In 1976 she was owned by Golden City Maritime Corporation Panama.[1]

1983 Broken up at Kaohsiung, Taiwan.[6]

Built 1956	**Yard No** 501
Specifications	
7984 Gross tons	
453 x 62 x 35 feet	
Machinery	
Diesel 8000BHP (B&W type) by J G Kincaid of Greenock. 6 Cyls 750mm Dia 2000mm stroke.	
16 knots	
Complement	
12 Passengers 74 Crew	

SS ALMERIAN

SS ALMERIAN was built for the Ellerman and Bucknall Shipping Co. She was the last steamship to be built on the Tay the first being built in 1814. On 3/1/57 at Izmir Turkey fire broke out amongst the cotton cargo in No5 tween decks. The cargo was destroyed but the ship was undamaged. The fire was extinguished by the crew in 20 minutes.

She grounded on rocks off Ras Ibn Hani on 27/1/58 while entering Lattakia (Syria) from Middlesborough. The Norwegian ship MV BAGHDAD grounded at same time. ALMERIAN had only 83 tons of cargo for Lattakia and Iskenderun on board. On February 10th 120 tons of bunker oil was transferred by barge to the Ellerman and Wilson liner CATTARO. Later 300 tons oil and cargo were transferred. She floated on 22/2/58 and BAGHDAD floated the same day. ALMERIAN took 350 tons of bunkers from SS ANDALUSIAN and sailed for Famagusta. Drydocked at Syra, Greece, for examination severe bottom damage was discovered. Repairs on the Tyne took 3 months.

Renamed CITY of LEEDS in 1962 and transferred to the Borneo-Sarawak service. Retransferred to Ellerman Meditteranean service in 1964 and renamed ALMERIAN. She was chartered for Cunard Lines' London to Great Lakes Service in 1966 Renamed ASSYRIA. Returned to Ellerman in November 1966 and renamed ALMERIAN. Again chartered for Cunard Great Lakes service in 1967 renamed ASIA.

Sold in Greece in November 1969 for £150,000 and renamed THECKLETOS the new owners being Ealection Shipping Co. Famagusta Cyprus. In 1973 owned by Melcoroma C A Nav, SA Panama under the Greek flag.

In 1973 she discharged a 141ton electrical transformer from Sweden at Toledo where two heavy lift gantry cranes were used. She was scrapped at Kaohsiung in 1974.[1]

Built 1956   **Yard No** 502

Specifications
3649 Gross tons
350 x 53 x 33 feet

Machinery
Steam triple expansion 3200 BHP with Baur Wach exhaust turbine by Central Marine Engine Works, West Hartlepool.
Cyls 23 38 65/48"
12 knots

Complement
0 Passengers 47 Crew

TSMV PHAROS

Dundee City Archives

TSMV PHAROS was built for the Commissioners of the Northern Lighthouse Board as a lighthouse tender.
This was a magnificent vessel with an outfit similar to a passenger cruise ship and was Flagship of the Commodore of the fleet.(DM)
She was badly damaged by fire at Troon on 20/8/63 when the crew were on leave and only a watchman aboard.
Ten cabins were gutted and the stern was white hot. The fire was extinguished after 3 hours after attendance of fire brigades from Troon Ardrossan and Ayr.[1]

Built 1955   **Yard No** 507

Specifications
1712 Gross tons
235 x 40 x 19 feet

Machinery
Diesel 1970 BHP 2 stroke by British Polar engines Glasgow.
7 Cyls 340mm Dia 570mm stroke

14 knots

Complement
23 Passengers 18 Crew

MV CANADIAN STAR

MV CANADIAN STAR was built for the Blue Star Line and had significant refrigeration capacity. Her maiden voyage was round the world to Suva, New Zealand and Australia via Panama and home via Suez. The Second voyage was the reverse. She struck the bottom off Arran in fog 14/1/58 en route Liverpool – Glasgow – Vancouver. There were 2500 tons part cargo on board and the bottom was badly damaged. She returned to Liverpool and then the Tyne for repairs. In February 1964 she loaded a record cargo of 1600 tons of binder and baler twine from Belfast Ropeworks for San Francisco, Portland, Seattle and Vancouver. In 1965 she transported 55 rollers each weighing 9 tons and of 20 feet in length for a paper manufacturing firm at Duncan Bay, Vancouver Island to which a special call was made.

In 1967 she was modified for whisky container traffic from Glasgow to the West Coat of North America (WCNA). Her capacity was 60 containers 20ft x 8ft x 8ft to conform to the International Standards Organisation. The containers were to be filled at the distilleries.

In 1971 she was transferred to Lamport and Holt services and renamed RAEBURN following the introduction of container ships to WCNA trade. At Porto Allegro on 30/1/74 a drum of chemicals struck the weather deck coaming during discharge. A rope sling had broken and the drum fell into the hold and burst. Decontamination took three days and involved the removal and burning of dunnage. In 1979 she was sold to owners Vertigo Shipping Co of Limassol. She was resold in 1979 to Taiwan breakers for $125 per ton light displacement. (5750 tons).[1]

1979 Vertigo Shipping Co., Ltd., Panama; Renamed BRAEBURN.
1979 Keun Hwa Iron Steel Works& Enterprise Ltd., Taiwan; Arrived at Kaohsiung to be broken up; Demolition Commenced.[6]

Built 1957   **Yard No** 508

Specifications
6291 Gross tons
 435 x 63 x 39 feet

Machinery
Diesel 8000 BHP (Doxford type) by Scotts of Greenock.
6 Cyls 725mm dia 2250 stroke comb.

 15.5 knots
Complement
12 Passengers   50 Crew

MV MENELAUS

MV MENELAUS was built for the Alfred Holt Co. Sister ship MENESTHEUS was built about the same time. On 8/2/58 she suffered slight damage to her bows in collision with the Russian MV LENA in Gladstone Dock Liverpool when arriving from Otaru, Japan. In 1966 she was evacuated at Liverpool due to a bomb scare but no trace was found. In 1972 transferred to the Elder Dempster Line and renamed MENO.
In 1972 she was renamed OTI. In 1978 sold to Thenemaris Maritime of Greece and registered as belonging to Palermo Shipping Co. being renamed ELSTAR. She was scrapped at Kaohsiung in 1979.[1]

MV MENESTHEUS was on fire while fitting out at the Caledon on 30/8/57 resulting in £300 electrical damage in the winch conductor house. Four fire engines were in attendance.
Slightly damaged in collision with the Russian SS STALINGRAD at Singapore 7/3/61 en route Hamburg to Manila. On 30/12/60 in the Bay of Biscay she witnessed an explosion from 16 miles away on the liner INDIAN NAVIGATOR which was then abandoned. She took off 47 of the 67 crew and the Dutch ship DALERDYJK took another 20. She landed at Liverpool on 1/1/61. On 2nd January the INDIAN NAVIGATOR blew up and sank with 13 prize crew from INDIAN SUCCESS.
On 9/9/76 she was in collision with MV CAP BON at Bremen en route Hamburg to Apapa, Nigeria. Damage was slight and she proceeded to Antwerp.
In 1977 she was transferred to Elder Dempster service and renamed ONITSHA. She was sold to Thenemaris Maritime of Greece in 1978 and registered as belonging to Leon Rivera Lines Co of Monrovia. She was scrapped at Kaohsiung in 1979.[1]
1978 Thenamaris Maritime Inc., Piraeus; re named ELISLAND but operated by Palrme Shipping Co., Cyprus.
1979 Arrived at Kaohsuing for breaking up Lung Fa Steel & Iron Co. Apr. 12 Demolition commenced.[6]

Built 1957   **Yard No** 509
Specifications
8539 Gross tons
455 x 65x 36 feet

Machinery
Diesel 8500BHP opposed piston (B&W type) by Harland & Wolff of Belfast.
6 Cyl 750mm dia 2000mm stroke comb.
17 knots

Complement
12 Passengers   76 Crew

MV TEMPLEMAIN

 Mr G Parker receives the launch-stage cheque

MV TEMPLEMAIN was built for the Temple Steamship Co of London.
Sold in 1969 to Cia Nav Sante Irene SA Panama for £395,000 renamed IRINI.[1]

Completed for Lambert Bros., Ltd as Managers.
1984 Spirit Shipping Co.,Ltd., Malta; Re named SPIRIT.
1984 Broken up at Gadani Beach, Pakistan, Prior to 8th June 1984.[6]

Built   1958   **Yard No** 511

Specifications
8005 Gross tons
425 x 58 x 38 feet

Machinery
Diesel 3300 BHP (Doxford type) by
Vickers Armstrong of Barrow.
4 Cyls 600mm dia 2320mm stroke

13 knots

Complement
0 Passengers   51 Crew

130

MV ELIZABETH BOWATER

MV ELIZABETH BOWATER.   While on passage London to Risor in December 1962 diverted in the North Atlantic to assist same owners LIVERPOOL PACKET disabled 53N 21W. Tow parted off Fastnet but reached Cobh 17/12/62.

In 1966 in collision at Nore anchorage on February 17th with the Norwegian tanker METCO causing superficial damage to the tanker.

In 1971 aground in Wando river Charleston Feb 21; refloated Feb22.

In 1972 sold to Wimpey Marine Ltd and renamed WIMPEY SEALAB. Taken to the Tyne for conversion to an oil rig drilling ship. In November 1972 she was chartered for preliminary survey work on the proposed channel tunnel route between Dover and Calais which involved drilling to 200 feet with a temporary 45 foot drilling rig in No3 hold working through a moonpool in the bottom. This took 4 months.

On 19/11/72 she was towed from Dover to Gravesend disabled with a wire round the screw by Bugsier tug HERMES. In 1973 she was chartered to the National Coal Board to spend 6 weeks drilling for coal off Northumberland. The aim was to prove further undersea coal resources for Lynemouth Ellington pit the world's biggest undersea mine. The job was to sink five undersea borehole to depths of 120 feet. On completion she returned to Shields for major conversion to an undersea research and geological vessel. The 45 foot drilling rig was replaced by a more sophisticated 120 foot rig and a computer controlled dynamic position centred system.

In Nov 1974 she was drilling in the Forth and helped to locate vast underground coal reserves off Musselburgh.[1]

Built 1958   Yard No 512 Other details as for CONSTANCE BOWATER (next page).

MV CONSTANCE BOWATER

Dundee City Archives

MV CONSTANCE BOWATER was built for the Bowater Steamship Co. for the transport of paper materials and products.

She had a specially strong bow for sailing through ice. Sister ship ELIZABETH BOWATER was built about the same time (see previous page).

After her maiden voyage from Sweden to Ellesmere Port with wood pulp she loaded an experimental cargo of 1250 tons pulpwood from Forestry commission estates in North Wales at Birkenhead for Risor Norway for processing in a new plant to see if suitable for installation in new plant at Ellesmere Port.

En route Corner Brook to Great Lakes May 1959. She struck No2 lock entering the Welland Canal Oct 19 1959 bound Newfoundland to Cleveland with newsprint.

Grounded outside Risor Mar 7 1963 en route Abo to Ellesmere Port causing a dent 30 feet long in the bilge keel and slight leaking. Discharged 400 tons of pulp damaged by salt water. Renamed KRETON SPIRIT in 1972 in ownership of Maria Victoria SA of Greece, registered in Monrovia.[1]

Strengthened for navigation in Ice. In 1985 renamed SIPSA and owned by Soc. Industrial de Productos Siderurgicis S.A.; Arrived Mamoal. Demolition began at Cartagena, Columbia. [6]

Built 1958	**Yard No** 513

Specifications
4045 Gross tons
310 x 50 x 30 feet

Machinery
Diesel 2700BHP SA by Wm Denny
Bros of Dumbarton (Sulzer type)
6 Cyl 600mm dia 1040mm stroke
12 knots

Complement
4 Passengers 38 Crew

MV CITY of HEREFORD

MV CITY of HEREFORD was built for Ellerman Lines.

In May 1969 she was chartered by the Karachi – UK Pakistan Shipping Lines at 21s per ton deadweight. (7610 tons deadweight).

On 29/4/1968 she had a fire in No1 hold en route Kota Kinabalu to London evidenced by smoke from a ventilator. The hatches were battened down and carbon dioxide injected. She arrived at Port Louis, Maurutius on April 30th and the tug WINNIE assisted with fire hoses the fire being brought under control by May 5th. 250 tons of copra cake were damaged by fire water. As cargo was well stowed and ventilated the fire was attributed to the "inherent vice" of copra cake. She sailed on May 11th.

Renamed CITY of GLASGOW in 1971. In 1978 renamed MYRNA and owned by Porter Shipping Co. of Monrovia. On 29/3/79 she was slightly damaged in collision with the Icelandic MV MULAFOSS at Gdynia.[1]

Delivered to Hall Line as Managers for Ellerman Lines Ltd.

1980 Left Manila for breaking up at Kaohsiung Taiwan.[6]

Built 1958   **Yard No** 514

Specifications
4954 Gross tons
405 x 59 x 37 feet

Machinery
Diesel 5040BHP Doxford type by G Clark
NEM of Sunderland 8 Cyls Dia 720mm
Stroke 1250mm Combined.
14 knots

Complement
0 Passengers   66 Crew

MV MACHAON

MV MACHAON was built for the Alfred Holt Company. Sister ship MARON was built about the same time. She was on fire in tween decks en route Glasgow to Manila and docked at Singapore 19/7/64. Renamed CHUOSI in 1977 and transferred to Elder Dempster service. Renamed MED ENDEAVOUR under ownership of Med Transport and Trading Corp. SA Panama, registered at Limassol.
She was scrapped at Kaohsiung in 1979.[1]

Blue Funnel Line, Managers.
1977 Elder Dempster Line; Re named OBUASI.
1978 Thenamaris Maritime Inc., Piraeus.; renamed ELSEA.
Passed immediately to Tartan Shipping Ltd., Monrovia to become MED ENDEAVOUR.[6]

Built 1959   **Yard No** 515

Specifications
8531 Gross tons
455 x 65 x 36feet

Machinery
Diesel 8500BHP 2 stroke by GJ Kincaid of
Greenock 6 Cyls Dia 750mm Stroke
2000mm total

16.5 knots

Complement
12 Passengers   78 Crew

MV BAHARISTAN

MV BAHARISTAN was built for the C Strick Shipping line for the transport of sugar and associated products. Her maiden voyage was UK – Persian Gulf - Canada – UK. She was 10,900 tons deadweight and 603,000 feet bale and at 15knots consumed 28 tons per day of intermediate fuel. She was chartered at $1500 per day for service from New York to Europe. In 1966 she was on charter to Ellerman at 10.000 deadweight on 32 tons fuel/day (probably heavy fuel oil [DM]) for service on the Calcutta/Chittagong/UK route. In 1973 under charter to Burma Five Star at 11,500 tons dead weight at 14knots on 24 tons fuel/day plus 1.5 tons diesel. The route was Rangoon to Europe at a rate of £1120 per day including overtime.

In 1975 she was renamed STRATHAROS on transfer to the P&O General Cargo division. She was sold to Pakistani scrappers in 1977 but resold to Chi Kong Co Inc of Monrovia, renamed CHI KONG, in 1978 being ultimately scrapped at Kaohsiung in 1979.[1]

1972 May 1st; P.& O. General Cargo Division appointed Managers.

1979 sold to Taiwan Ship Scrap Co., Ltd., demolition commenced at Kaohsiung,Taiwan.[6]

Built   1959   **Yard No** 516

Specifications
8517 Gross tons
530 x 72 x 39 feet

Machinery
Diesel 6500BHP (Doxford type) by
Hawthorn Leslie of Newcastle upon Tyne
6 Cyls Dia 670 Stroke 2320mm combined.

15 knots

Complement
4 Passengers   82 Crew

MV ATHELPRINCE

MV ATHELPRINCE was built for the Athel line a subsidiary of United Molasses of London. Sister ship ATHELPRINCESS was built about the same time. She loaded grain at Great Lakes completing Montreal in November 1960. Bound for Hull she grounded at Batiscan 23/11/60 between Montreal and Quebec after a steering gear failure but refloated quickly apparently undamaged. She was lengthened by 50 feet at Copenhagen giving a new tonnage of 11,687. In 1966 she was transferred to the Sugar Line and renamed SUGAR IMPORTER. In 1968 new owners were Albion Co Ltd. In 1976 she was sold to South American Interests for $2,200,000 and renamed LUCKY IMPORTER under ownership of Inter Bulkers Inc Panama. On 18/2/77 bound for San Nicholas (Argentine) with coal she was aground in the Martin Garcia channel in the river Plate but refloated on February 21st after lightening of 4000 tons. On 20/10/78 she was aground entering Mare del Plata from Baton Rouge with fertliser but refloated after 10 hours. Owned by Wallem Ship Management in 1979.[1]
Broken up 1983. [6]

MV ATHELPRINCESS She loaded 11,000 tons bulk wheat from a silo at Melbourne in 10 hours in July 1961. She was lengthened by 50 feet at Copenhagen in 1965 with new tonnage of 11687. She arrived at Auckland on 15/6/65 from Coatzacoolcas and reported that seawater had contaminated her cargo of sulphur.
In 1966 she was transferred to the Sugar Line Ltd and renamed SUGAR EXPORTER.
In 1968 owned by Albion Co Ltd. She was on charter to a Dutch firm at 16,160 tons deadweight 634,229 grain, 14knots on 32 tons per day plus 1 ton diesel, geared as a bulk carrier for $6700 (per day) plus $1000 a month overtime with delivery at Gravesend and redelivery at Indonesia. In 1976 she was sold in Greece and renamed ZEUS.[1]
1980 Nickolaos Shipping Inc. Greece; European Navigation Inc., Managers; renamed NICKOLAS K.; Port of Registry Piraeus.
1982 Coombe Shipping Corp (European Navigation Inc.) of Panama; renamed DEVON; Port of Registry Panama.
1983 Maritime Factors Inc., Philippines; became BANAHAW. [1]
1985 Arrived at Dalien, China to be broken up; resold to Chinese Shipbreakers.[6]

Built 1959	Yard No 517

Specifications
10,295 Gross tons
455 x 63 x 39 feet

Machinery
Diesel 5500BHP 2 stroke by Hawthorn Leslie of Newcastle upon Tyne 5 Cyls Dia 670mm Stroke 2320mm combined.
14 knots

Complement
0 Passengers   55 Crew

MV CITY of DUNDEE

Dundee City Archives

MV CITY of DUNDEE was built for the Ellerman & Bucknall Steamship Company of Hull. Sister ship CITY of WORCESTER was built about the same time.

Jute in No2 hold was seriously on fire at King George Wharf Dundee 4/2/64. The fire was stifled with CO2 injection. The ship was undamaged but there was £45,000 fire and water damage to the cargo of jute and mica. The fire was caused by a wire chain sparking off hatch coamings. In 1978 she was renamed DUNDEE under ownership of Dundee Maritime Co of Limassol.[1]

1971 Jan 1st Became part of Ellerman City Liners Fleet

1980 Kilkis Navagation Co., Cyprus. Owned by Lifedream Cica Naviera, Limassol; Became CITY OF DUNDEE. 1982 Repairs required. Class suspended. [L.R. 1983]

1984 Arrived Gadani Beach, Pakistan, and broken up there by Panama Shipbreaking Co.[6]

CITY of WORCESTER On fire in No3 tween deck at Avonmouth on 27/6/77 bound Cochin to Manchester. Renamed in 1979 MARIA DIAMATOS under ownership of Vermont SS Co of Piraeus.[1]

Delivered to the Hall Line.

1982 Seaost Navigation Co., Cyprus; renamed CAPE GRECO Port of Registry Limmasol.

1982 Laid up at Djibouti with engine failure.

1983 sold to Ashraf Bros for breaking up; Run onto Fouzderhat Beach Chittagong and broken up.[6]

Built 1961   **Yard No** 529

Specifications
7149 Gross tons
405 x 59 x 37 feet

Machinery
Diesel 5600 HP by G Clark NEM of
Sunderland Cyls 720mm Stroke 1250mm.

14 knots

Complement
0 Passengers   68 Crew

MV NINA BOWATER

MV NINA BOWATER was built for the Bowater shipping Co.
Sold in 1977 to the Liberian Corporation for $1 million for registry under the Greek flag and renamed KRETAN GLORY owned by Maria Victoria Nav SA Piraeus.[1]

Cayzer, Irvine & co.,Ltd. Managers.
1977 Martima Kretan Glory S.A.; Maria Victoria Naviera S.A., Panama , Managers; renamed KRETAN GLORY. Port of Registry Piraeus.
1982 Admiralty International Shipping Ltd., Panama; renamed PROMETHEUS V Port of registry Panama; Seatrans Brokerage Inc., Managers.
Left Monfalcone Italy in tow 3/9/86 and arrived at Porto Nogaro about 4/9/86 for breaking up.
1987 Sold to Italian Breakers.[6]

Built 1961   **Yard No** 530

Specifications
4017 Gross tons
310 x 50 x 30 feet

Machinery
Diesel 3000 BHP Sulzer SA 2 stroke
6SD60
6Cyl Dia 600mm Stroke 1040mm

 14 knots

Complement
4 Passengers   38 Crew

TSMV POLE STAR

TSMV POLE STAR was built for the Northern Lighthouse Board Commissioners as a lighthouse tender. On 3/3/62 her crew located a drifting motor boat 9 miles off N Ronaldsay Lighthouse being the mailboat ISLAND LASS which was taken in tow but sank in bad weather. Five men had been taken off the boat by a trawler in a blizzard two days before.

Flannon Islands lighthouse was automated April 5 1971 and POLE STAR took three keepers off for the last time on 27/9/71. The islands are totally uninhabited.[1]

Built   1961   **Yard No** 531

Specifications
1328 Gross tons
215 x 40 x 18 feet

Machinery
Diesel twin 1920HP by British Polar of Glasgow SA 2 stroke
2 x 6 Cyl Dia 340mm Stroke 540mm

14 knots

Complement
36 Passengers   38 Crew

MV NGAKUTA

MV NGAKUTA was built for the Union Steamship Co of New Zealand as a newsprint carrier. Sister ship NGATORO was built about the same time.

MV NGAKUTA She ran aground at Tauranga entrance but was floated, undamaged, with assistance on the next tide after discharge of part cargo into a lighter.[1]

Built for carrying forest products across the Tasman Sea.

1983 Giant Ocean Shipping S.A. Panamanian Flag; renamed GIANT TREASURE Port of Registry Panama.

1986 Sold to Reach Ocean Shipping S.A. of Taiwan. Panamanian Flag; renamed RICHER Port of Registry Panama.

1992 Abandoned in South China Sea after taking water. On voyage from Fangcheng to Muara with cargo of cement. Last seen with decks awash Pos Lat. 10.24'N., Long.112'E.[6]

MV NGATORO On 26/4/63 she grounded in the channel leaving Tauranga for Sydney but floated undamaged. Renamed FLORENTIA 1976 under ownership of Flarvik Cia Nav SA of Panama but Pireaus based. Renamed KAPATAN ANTONIS. Owned in1978 by Ippocampus Maritime (Helles) Ltd Piraeus.[1]

1976 Florvik Compania Naviera S.A. Of Panama; Re named FLORENTIA Registered under Greek Flag, Registered at Piraeus.

1977 Ippocampos Maritime [Hellas] Lte., Greece; renamed KAPETAN ANTONIS Port of Registry Piraeus.

1988 Eastern Queen Co., S.A. Greece; Name Unchanged.

1991 Fadel Shipping Co., Lebanon; General United Trading & Shipping Co., S.A.R.L. Manahers; renamed FADELG Port of Registry Tripoli.

1996 sold to Indian Shipbreakers. Anchored off Alang for breaking.

Built 1962	**Yard No** 532

Specifications
4576 Gross tons
340 x 53x 29 feet

Machinery
Diesel 3000HP Denny Sulzer 6SD60
Dia 600mm Stroke 1040mm
14 knots

Complement
0 Passengers   38 Crew

MV BENARTY

MV BENARTY was built for Ben Line Steamers Ltd of Leith (Managers Thomson Shipping.) Typical voyage London to Hong Kong 30/8/64 to 30/10/64 (2).

Her first master was Capt Charles Donnelly of West Ferry. She was a heavy lift ship with Stulcken mast of 180 tons capacity. On 13/8/64 a fire was discovered aboard at Hull deep seated in copra. An automatic smoke alarm gave warning of fire in the forehold. 180 tons of 500 tons were discharged overside to lighters.

On 20/11/1965 she was aground at Barrow Deep (Thames estuary) bound London-Middlesborough and refloated same day with assistance of tug SUNXVII. On 29/8/69 there was a fire in No3 hold at Hamburg arriving from Kaohsiung. The cargo in the affected hold was cotton yarn, plastic toys, leather goods, plywood, preserves and gloves. The fire was smouldering among gloves and was fought with soda acid extinguishers. The ship was undamaged ,

On 12/5/72 she was in collision with American cargo ship JOHN LYKES off Krautsand Elbe. Both were inward bound and continued to Hamburg. BENARTY was leaking in No2 hold and drydocked on May 13 where 130 tons of steel were required for repairs. Damage to the other ship required 14 plates. In 1975 she brought a 101 ton locomotive and 34 ton tender from Rotterdam to Hull it having been bought from German Railways by the Steamtown Railway museum of Carnforth. Built in Berlin in 1940 it was converted to oil firing in 1967. It was 15 feet high and 80 feet long compared with 13 feet high and 74 feet long of Flying Scotsman also at Carnforth.

1979 April the ship was fined 8000 Francs at Havre for contravening shipping lane rules off Ushant. (In 1995 she loaded 12x 60 ton drums of 3.5 inch wire rope at Grangemouth for Japan, believed largest export order of its kind. It was to be used for anchor lines on the largest semi-submersible drilling rig building for Odeco.)

In 1995 she loaded a 167 ton pressure vessel 199 feet long at Middlesborough for Yosu S Korea for a British designed methanol plant. She grounded entering San Juan Puerto Rico 2 July 1970, bound Manila – Grangemouth, to land injured crew member. [1]

1981 Owned by Pacific International Lines [Pte] Ltd., Singapore; Re named KOTA PETANI Port of Registry Singapore. 1985 Arrived at Kaohsiung, Taiwan for breaking up.[6]

Built 1962	**Yard No** 534

Specifications
10,296 Gross tons
465 x 66 x 42 feet

Machinery
Diesel 9000 HP Fairfield-Rowan Sulzer
6RD76 6Cyl Dia 760mm Stroke1550mm

15 knots

Complement
0 Passengers   67 Crew

DHT No 8

DHT No8 was built for the Dundee Harbour Trust as a hopper barge.
Restricted to river Tay and within 10 miles of Buddon Ness. In 1975 Transferred to Dundee Port Authority.[1]

Built 1961	**Yard No** 535

Specifications
268 Gross tons
109 x 29 x 10 feet

Machinery
No propulsion

FERRY JOHN BURNS

Motor Ferry JOHN BURNS was built for the London County Council for the Thames crossing at Woolwich, London. Sister ships ERNEST BEVIN and JAMES NEWMAN were built about the same time.

She was built to carry 200 tons of vehicles and 1000 passengers and had Voith Schneider propellers.. The three ferries cost £804,000 and replaced 4 boats built 1922-30. The first free ferry was in 1889 but a service had been in existence since 1308. In 1978 she was struck by the suction dredger HOVERINGHAM VI and incurred side damage.

ERNEST BEVIN On 28/8/1968 an articulated lorry rolled forward and fell 12 feet to lower deck and the service was reduced to one ship.

JAMES NEWMAN In 1964 she was damaged when struck by the collier DAME CAROLINE HASLETT which was making to berth at Woolwich Power Station. Her bow plates were buckled and her loading ramp torn. Traffic was diverted by the tunnels but the ship was back in service in 2 hours.

The Woolwich Free Ferries were subsidised to the tune of £336,000 per year. The charge used to be one penny for the 12 minute crossing. They carry 1.2 million cars and 323,000 lorries per year and each boat operates 16 hours per day, 7 days per week.[1] In service at time of writing (2008).

Built 1963   **Yard No** 536

Specifications
739 Gross tons
184 x 61x 17 feet

Machinery
Twin Diesel 500 BHP Mirlees National
RHAUM7 4 stroke Cyls Dia 9" Stroke 12"

8.5 knots

Complement
1030 Passengers   22 Crew

MV PARTHIA

Dundee City Archives

MV PARTHIA was built for the Cunard Steamship Co of Southampton. Sister ship IVERNIA was built about the same time. Cunard –Brocklebank Ltd., Managers; for North Atlantic Cargo Service

In 1963 there was a fire in the refrigerated hold while fitting out at Caledon Jetty. On 23/2/1966 the steering gear was carried away 360 miles ESE of St Johns (NF) en route New York to London with general cargo. She was travelling at 17.5 knots in a 50 knot wind gusting to 60 and 15 foot seas with snow. The steering flat was an indescribable shambles, she lost her rudder and the stern frame was damaged. The tug FOUNDATION VIGILANT took over on 27 February 1050 miles East of Halifax. Under her skipper Capt Hehir she arrived at Southampton pm March 11th and was berthed by 4 local tugs. She had used her own main engines during the tow and made up to 9 knots. The propeller was damaged, some shell plates were torn and internals distorted. She was out of action for several months. In Sept 1969 she took her first container shipment of Irish Whiskey from Liverpool to New York. The container had two stainless steel tanks with 4500 gallons consigned to Peoria Illinois.

In 1971 she was sold to the Western Australian Coastal Shipping Commission along with MEDIA (Tyne built) for £1,400,000 for the two. Renamed WAMBIRI in Aug 1971 and renamed in 1979 RICE TRADER under Greek ownership.[1]

1984 Engine failure off Socotra. Towed into Djibouti. Left in tow for Karachi.

Scrapped at Gadani Beach.[6]

IVERNIA   In Feb 1968 loaded up a Ferranti, Hollinwood, 140 ton transformer bound Liverpool to New York for Niagra Power Station. Lift was by the floating crane MAMMOTH. On 21/8/69 there were loaded at Liverpool for New York 2 Pullman cars, an exhibition coach plus an administration car for the Flying Scotsman nine coach whistle stop exhibition trip from New York to Houston. In 1970 she was lengthened by 80 feet at the Swan Hunter yard on the Tyne increasing her capacity by 2000 tons. Transferred to Brocklebank Service as MANIPUR . In 1971 renamed CONCORDIA MANIPUR and later that year reverted to MANIPUR. In 1974 dockers refused to load sugar for Saudi Arabia at Hull due to UK shortage.

She was laid up at Falmouth in Sept 1977 along with three other Cunard-Brocklebank liners pending disposal. In 1978 she was owned by the Mediterranean Navigation Co. and renamed PHILLIPA. .[1]

1985 At Chittagong for Scrapping by Ranman Shipbreakers.[6]

Built 1963	**Yard No** 539

Specifications
5586 Gross tons
400 x 60 x 37 feet

Machinery
Diesel 7700 BHP John Brown Sulzer
7RD68 2 stroke SA
7Cyl Dia680mm Stroke1250mm
16 knots
Complement
0 Passengers   43 Crew

144

MV PORT HUON

Dundee City Archives

MV PORT HUON was built for the Port line of Southampton for the transport refrigerated cargo. Sister ship PORT ALBANY was also built about the same time.

PORT HUON was the last ship launched with G. Parker as the Caledon S&E Co. Managing Director. PORT ALBANY was the first ship with T. Parnell as MD.[2]

PORT HUON 1964 #541 There was a slight fire in the refrigeration section while fitting out on 24/1/65. In 1972 renamed JULIETTA, Liberian flag, owned by Afromer Inc Piraeus.

In 1974 operating for the Argentinian ELMA line sailing London to Buenos Aires.

1975 registered at Limassol.[1]

Ownership moved to Port Line; transferred to Blue Star Port Lines Management.

1971 Group Ownership passed to Trafalgar House Investments Ltd.

1984 Egyptian Reefer & General Cargo Shipping Co., S.A. Egypt; renamed AMANA; Port of Registry Alexandria.

1992 Laid up at Piraeus.

1993 Universal Ltd., St. Vincent; Managers Incom Shipping Ltd. St Vincent.

1994 Sold to Indian Shipbreakers at Alang. Arrived there 31.1.94. Beached there for breaking up.[6]

PORT ALBANY On 7/2/1967 bound for Brisbane cargo broke loose between Halifax to New York in heavy weather causing internal damage in No 3 upper tween deck. On 13/1/68 bound Melbourne to New York she grounded in mud 25 feet off the dock at Houston while fully laden with frozen meat but floated 13/1 with no damage. Renamed MARIETTA in 1992 under Liberian Flag owners Afromer Inc Pireaus. 1975 registered at Limassol.[1]

1990 Greek Regular Lines Special Shipping Co., Inc., Greece; Re named ARTEMON.

1992 Sold to Indian Shipbreakers Arrived at Alang to be broken up.

Built 1964	**Yard No** 541

Specifications
8493 Gross tons
450 x 67 x 40 feet

Machinery
Diesel 12000 BHP by Wallsend Slipway
at Wallsend
2-stroke 8 Cyl Dia 760mm Stroke 1550mm

19 knots

Complement
 0 Passengers   58 Crew

MV NGAHERE

MV NGAHERE was built for the Union steamship Co of New Zealand for the transport of newsprint. Sister ship NGAPARA was built about the same time.

In 1977 17 members of crew were arrested at Lautoka charged with obstructing the police. They refused to move the vessel from the wharf during a labour dispute to allow another vessel to have its berth. Fined 80 Fijian dollars.[1]

1987 Foojadi Shipping Co.,Ltd., Maldives; renamed SEA HORSE Port of registry Male.

1999 Sold to Indian breakers. Arrived at Mumbai [Bombay] for demolition.[6]

MV NGAPARA 1986 Sold to Reach Shipping S.A. Panama; renamed KENT BRILLIANT Port of Registry Panama.

1993 Renamed FINANCIER for final voyage. Sold for scrap. Arrived in tow at Keelung after losing her rudder. Subsequently towed to Hong Kong sold to Chinese breakers; Arrived at Huangpu in tow for scrapping.[6]

Built 1966	**Yard No** 543

Specifications
4543 Gross tons
340 x 53 x 29 feet

Machinery
Diesel 3285 BHP by British Polar of Glasgow
6 Cyls Dia 500mm Stroke 700mm

14 knots

Complement
0 Passengers 39 Crew

TSMV BEXLEY

Dundee City Archives

TSMV BEXLEY was built for the London County Council as a sludge tanker. Sister ships NEWHAM, and HOUNSLOW were built about the same time.

Built for a contract price of £529,000. Sludge from treatment works at Beckton and Crossness was dumped at Barrow Deep 55 miles out of London. On 24/1/72 the ship PANDO SOUND passed at speed causing three ropes to part at Beckton and approximately 200 tons of sludge spilled into the Thames. In 1975 owners became Thames Water Board. On 8/1/77 she stood by coaster ROSEMARKIE aground at West Barrow Sands Thames estuary.[1]

NEWHAM   On 10/1/67 in collision in the Thames with MV RIVKA outward bound to Malta and Haifa. Newham was at Black Deep, South Cutfell.

Other ship put back with stern damage and Newham incurred bad damage to port bridge wing and port bulwarks. In 1975 owners were Thames Water Board.[1]

1998 Thames Water Authority; Managers; Crescent Ship Management Ltd.

1998 Withdrawn from service and laid up; European Union Regulations forbid dumping sewage waste at sea

1998 Madeline Maritime S.A., Panama; Port of Registry San Lorenzo [Honduras].

2000 Class deleted from Lloyds, Vessel to be broken up.

2001 Sold by unspecified Honduras Flag Interest to Indian Breakers.[6]

Built 1966	**Yard No** 545

Specifications
2175 Gross tons
280 x 48 x 18 feet

Machinery
Twin Diesel   2756 BHP total
Ruston Hornsby of Lincoln type 6ATCM
Twin gearboxes 6 Cyls Dia 12.5" Stroke 14.5"

12 knots

Complement
0 Passengers   28 Crew

MV LYMINGE

Dundee City Archives

MV LYMINGE was built for R B Constants Ltd for bulk cargo duties.
On 26/11/67 she suffered engine trouble at 39.16N 29.10 W while en route Aviles-Claymont. Towed to Ponta Delgada on 27/11/97. The cause was shaft gearbox trouble. Towed to Falmouth for repairs. In 1969 bound Antwerp to Chicago with steel she put into St Johns NF on 14 June with generator trouble. On 24/7/69 arrived at Pesages from Chicago with scavenger pump trouble.
26/11/70 Towed 12 miles to Falmouth by tug PACIFIC after a crankcase explosion.
1975 Sold to Yugoslavian owners for $3 million, renamed KROPENJ, and owned by Slobodna Plovidba of Sibenik, Later owned by Theodoros Konidaris & Palmis of Pireaus.[1]

Built 1967   **Yard No** 547

Specifications
4980 Gross tons
375 x 54 x 29 feet

Machinery
Diesel 4000HP by British Polar Glasgow.
Geared 10 Cyls Dia 500mm Stroke 700mm

14 knots

Complement
0 Passengers 32 Crew

MV LUISE BORNHOFEN

MV LUISE BORNHOFEN was built for Robert Bornhofen Reederi of Hamburg.

1968 9050 tons deadweight 17-17.5 knot on 28 tons/fuel/day max $1850 per day owner's option 7400 12 months time charter Lloyd Brasiliero April-May.

1971 – 9200 tons dw 17.5knots on 29 tons/day max + 2 tons diesel $1450 /day Heure–W Indies KNSM Aug.

22/12/1972 In collision at Weser with 400 ton dw river vessel ODER. ODER sank immediately. Three men crew saved in lifeboat. LUISE BORNHOFEN bound Milwaukee – Hamburg – Bremen. Slight damage.

1973 Renamed LUISE Liberian flag 6377 gross owners Hanover Shipping Co Ltd Monrovia.

Renamed ATLANTICO in 1975 owners Meresia SA Barcelona.

Arrived Bilbao from Valparaiso 7/1/78 after a fire in No2 hold on passage. Believed to be due to spontaneous combustion of fish meal while on passage and extinguished using CO2. It flared up later and was still burning on arrival at Bilbao and extinguished by fire brigade. Beans for Lisbon and fish meal for Leghorn were damaged the latter being dumped at sea.

On 31/8/78 she was in collision near Gibraltar from Panama with a RoRo ship JOLLY AZZUIRO which sank. ATLANTICO towed to Algericas by tug WOTAN after picking up 12 survivors.[1]

Built 1967   **Yard No** 548

Specifications
6380 Gross tons
395 x 61 x 35 feet

Machinery
Diesel 8400 BHP by MAN of Augsburg
type K6Z
6 cyl   Dia 700mm   Stroke 1200mm

17 knots

Complement
0 Passengers   38 Crew

MV MAHENO

MV MAHENO was built for the Union steamship Co of New Zealand. Sister ship MARAMA was also built at this time. These were the last ships built by the Caledon Co before it became Robb-Caledon.
In June 1968 on trials she had gearbox trouble which delayed delivery for 6 weeks. Maiden voyage of 11,460 miles Dundee to Auckland 6/11/68 took 28 days and made an average of 17.5 knots.
6/11/75 Held up at Auckland when the crew refused to open aft loading door as part of a protest over time off and holiday pay. Bound Lyttleton Wellington Touranga and Adelaide.
1/12/76 Renamed JOLLY GIALLO and owned by Thames Marine Panama for trading in the Mediterranean area.. 1978 Trading Italy –Apapa –Lagos.[1]

MV MARAMA Vehicular and Container Ro.Ro. Stern Loading Ferry.
MARAMA Launch postponed on 5/3/69 due to a shipwrights strike.
Launched later in fog with no ceremony.
Sold to Ascot shipping NZ 1976 for $7.2 Million and chartered back to the Union company and remained on the NZ- Aus liner service.[1]
Ran Trials off St.Abb's Head Speed 19.25 knots.
1984 Laid up at Wellington.
1984 Ascot Shipping Ltd., Panama; Renamed MARADA.
Later sold to Trident Transportation Co., Panama; name unchanged; remained laid up.
1985 Came out of lay-up for final voyage to Kaohsiung. Arrived at Kaohsiung for breaking up.[6]

MARAMA was the last ship built under Caledon S&E Ltd management. Remaining ships would be by Robb-Caledon Ltd.

Built 1969   **Yard No** 551

Specifications
4510 Gross tons
400 x 63 x 40 feet

Machinery
Twin Diesel   13020 BHP total by Crossley Premier of Manchester 4 stroke 14 cylinders Dia 400mm Stroke 460mm

18 knots

Complement
0 Passengers   35 Crew

MV SUVARNABHUMI

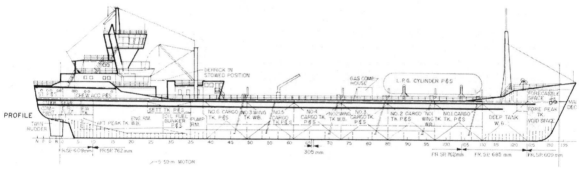

MV SUVARNABHUMI was built for the Thai Petroleum Transport Co. as a tanker.
She was the first ship built at Dundee under British Shipbuilders' Robb Caledon management resulting from
the reorganization and nationalization of British Shipbuilding.

Built 1969   **Yard No** 553

Specifications
3138 Gross tons
320 x 49 x 23 feet

Machinery
Diesel 1450 BHP by English Electric
(Ruston) of Newton Le Willows
type 8CSUM 8 Cylinder and gearbox.
Cyls Dia 10" Stroke 12"

12 knots

Complement
0 Passengers 22 Crew

MV CITY of LIVERPOOL

MV CITY of LIVERPOOL was built for the Ellerman Bucknall Line. Sister ship CITY of HULL was built about the same time. Achieved 20.5 kn on trials. Maiden voyage London-Continent – S Africa and on final leg of return voyage to Hull and Rotterdam was in collision 5m from Humber with Norwegian MV JORK 1.30 am on 8/12/70. 14 men from JORK taken off by Finnish MV MIRA. Master and 4 men reboarded ship when she did not sink. Spurn lifeboat took 9 men from MIRA. CITY of LIVERPOOL with bow and stern damage stood by till JORK taken in tow by tug FOREMAN. JORK bound Immingham – Naples with 1650 tons of coke towed back to Immingham.

25/8/71 Plates set due to collision with Quay when berthing at Laurenco Marques in a strong wind. 23/12/73 Fire in No2 hold at Calcutta loading for St John (NB) and extinguished in two hours with CO2. Water had been unsuccessful. Hatch left sealed. Cargo in hold was 1135 baled gunnies, 300 cases of tea. No structural damage.[1]

Delivered to Ellerman & Bucknell as Managers.

1981 Sun Horizon Nav. A.A., Piraaeus; Managers Diana shipping Agencies S.A.

Aground off Turks Island , but refloated 10 days later.

1986 Arrived at Kaohsiung, Taiwan and broken up.[6]

MV CITY of HULL Arrived back in UK in April 1974 for first time since maiden voyage to Persian gulf and had been on the Canada-India trade. Capt F Smith was presented with a plaque with the Hull City coat of arms at Hull.

In 1974 Tug RAIYAN capsized and sank at Doha in 30 ft water 40 feet from the wharf. While attempting to tow CITY of HULL from berth.[1]

1980 Waveney Shipping Corp., Liberia, Greek Owned; Renamed St JOHN Port of registry Piraeus. Changed hands several times.

1995 Mortimer Shipping Corporation, St. Vincent; renamed MAGDELENA.

1996 Sold to Indian Breakers. Arrived at Alang for Breaking up.[6]

Built 1970	**Yard No** 554

Specifications
9767 Gross tons
470 x 72 x 41 feet

Machinery
Diesel   17,500 BHP by Doxford of
Sunderland type 76J7
Opposed piston, 7 cylinders Dia 760mm
Stroke 2180 combined.
19 knots

Complement
0 Passengers   55 Crew

MV JON RAMSOY

MV JON RAMSOY (Ship No 557, pictured) was built for Fluvial Et Maritime of Oslo for tanker duties. Sister ship PORT ANNA was built about the same time.
1972 Speed 15 knots nominal but made 16.2 on trials. 14 main tanks and 10 wing tanks. Sold in 1974 for 43million Norwegian Kroner ($7.67 million) to Hall Shipping Co of Montreal. Renamed DEAN TRANSPORT. In 1975 Owners were Scotia Toronto Dominion Leasing Ltd Toronto.[1]

MV PORT ANNA (No 556) Aground on the South Channel bank after leaving Donges , France on 28/2/72 with a full cargo of fuel oil for Lorient and floated next tide with three tugs.[1]

Built 1972   **Yard No** 557

Specifications
6304 Gross tons
120 x 19 x 10.5 metres

Machinery
Diesel   6000 BHP by Crossley SEMT
Pielstick type 12PC2V Unidirectional
12 Cyls Dia 400mm Stroke 460mm

15 knots

Complement
0 Passengers   31 Crew

MV IDA LUNDRIGAN

MV IDA LUNDRIGAN was built for Common Bros. (Management) Ltd. As a newsprint carrier. Sister ship RIA JEAN McMURTY was built about the same time.

IDA LUNDRIGAN 1972 #578 In Sept 1973 surveyed in dry dock at Hamburg for ice damage after grounding on March 15 and heavy wethaer damage on May 2 bound Genoa- Newcastle (NB).

12/75 Damaged a timber wharf at Chatham (NB) while berthing during a snowstorm.

1976 Transferred to Chima Shipping Ltd under the Canadian Flag and renamed A C CROSBIE . 12/9/1976 On fire in No2 hold while loading for Arctic at Montreal. Hold resealed and CO_2 injected; pumped in without success. After 2 days moved to Contrecoul 20 miles downstream. All cargo in holds discharged by shore grabs amounting to 667 tons bagged calcium oxide, 82 tons cement blocks 574 tons calcium sulphate, calcium chloride, plasterboard and 5 containers of household goods. All useless except 4 containers. Dept of Trade ordered removal of bagged calcium from No3 hold for containerisation. 2/10/76 While discharging containers at Strathcona (NW territories) two twelve ton cranes collapsed doing extensive damage. No other cranes available.

14/2/1977 Machinery damage while bound for Seven Islands. Another ship belonging to Chima shipping tried to tow but was unable to make headway through ice. Tug POINTE MARGUERITE was engaged to tow to Halifax. Slow speed owing to ice conditions.[1]

Completed Speed on trials. 17.185 knots off Burntisland.

Chartered to Newfoundland Pulp and Chemical Co.

1977 Sold to Chima Shipping Ltd[Crosbie & Co.,Ltd., Managers] Canada.

Changed ownership several times till 1998 Red Moon Shipping Co.; Bogazzio Servigi Navali Sri., Viareggio, Italy Managers.

1999 sold to Indian shipbreakers.

2000 Arrived Mumbai [Bombay] for Demolition.[6]

Built 1972	**Yard No** 558

Specifications
7100 Gross tons
114 x 19 x 11 metres

Machinery
Diesel 7000BHP by Crossley SEMT
Pielstick type 14PC2V Unidirectional.
14 Cyl 400 Dia 480 Stroke
15 knots

Complement
0 Passengers   38 Crew

154

FERRY CAEDMON

Motor Ferry CAEDMON was built for the British Rail Board for the Lymington to Isle of Wight ferry crossing.
Sister ships CENWULF and CENRED were also built about the same time.
For Isle of Wight services Portsmouth to Fishbourne and Lymington to Yarmouth. Mezannine decks installed
above car decks 1977-8 increasing car capacity by 20.
1978 Approx 500,000cars and 70,000 haulage vehicles annually.[1]

In service at time of writing (2008).

Built   1973   **Yard No** 560

Specifications
764 Gross tons
55 x 15.2 x 3.4 metres

Machinery
Diesel   990 BHP by Mirrlees Blackstone
of Stockport type 6ERS6M
twin 6 cyl Dia 8.7" Stroke 8.75"

11 knots

Complement
 Passengers   11 Crew

CRANE BARGE DP-ZS-1

Crane Barge was built for Navimor of Poland. The UK customer was Clarke Chapman – John Thompson – Cowans Sheldon.[2]
FLOATING CRANE Sub Contract from Clarke Chapman – John Thompson Group valued at £300,000. Crane superstructure was in position before launch. Designed for handling bulk cargoes. Four different kinds of grab. Primary duty is to unload large bulk cargo ore carriers in deep water off Szczecin, in the Oder estuary Poland. Max capacity of crane was 16 tons and could lift 550 tons per hour. Self propelled with full living accommodation.[1]

Built   1974   **Yard No** 563

Specifications
 646 Gross tons
36.6 x 16.75 x 3.66 metres

Machinery
Diesel twin English Electric
6 cyl dia 178mm stroke197mm

6 knots

Complement
0 Passengers   6 Crew

CS MONARCH

Dundee City Archives

CS MONARCH, a cable repair ship, was built for The British Post Office. Sister ship IRIS was built about the same time.
She had a crew of 63 and achieved 15.8 knots on trials. She laid cables in gales of force 8-9 while previous ships had been unable to work above force 4-5. MONARCH is a traditional cable ship name. An earlier ship of this name of 1122 tons was built at Port Glasgow and mined off Folkestone 8/9/1915.
CS IRIS was at the Silver Jubilee Review Spithead June 1977.

Built 1975   **Yard No** 564

Specifications
3874 Gross tons
84.2 x 15 x 8.8 metres

Machinery
Diesel twin 5200 BHP total by British
Polar Glasgow type SF116VS-E SA
4 stroke 16Cyl Dia 250mm Stroke 300mm
Both geared to single prop.
11 knots

Complement
0 Passengers   65 Crew

MV SALTA

 MV JUJUY II

MV SALTA was built for Empresa Lineas Maritimas Argentinas of Buenos Aires. Sister ships
JUJUY II and TUCUMAN were built about the same time.
She was a SD – 14 {a standard ship design} built under license. Engines by Doxford of Sunderland
Ran Trials off Burntisland. Speed 16.71 knots.
1995 sold to Container & Bulk Ltd., Malta; P & P Shipping Co., Piraeus Managers; renamed SEA DUKE Port
of Registry Valetta. (Malta)
2000 sold to Bangladesh breakers 2001 and arrived at Chittagong for demolition.[6]

Built   1977   **Yard No** 568

Specifications
9236 Gross tons
134 x 20.4 x 11.7 metres

Machinery
Diesel 8000BHP by Doxford of
Sunderland 4 Cyl Dia 670mm Stroke 2140
comb. Type M67J4   SA 2 stroke

16 knots

Complement
6 Passengers   39 Crew

158

MV GOLDEN BAY

MV GOLDEN BAY was built for Blue Circle Cement Co.as a bulk cement carrier.

The Golden Bay Cement Company's supply ship, MV Golden Bay, maintains silo levels at five ports around New Zealand. Cement is bagged at various Service Centres for export and domestic customers. [Company website current 2007]

Built 1979   **Yard No** 572

Specifications
3175 Gross tons
91.5 x 16.3 x 7.4 metres

Machinery
Diesel twin 4800 BHP total by Ruston of Newton le Willows type 12RKCM
12Cyl Dia 254mm Stroke 305mm

14 knots

Complement
0 Passengers   19 Crew

159

MV KOSCIERZYNA

MV KOSCIERZYNA was built for Polska Zegluga Morska (Polish Steamship Company) under the Anglo-Polish Shipping Venture as a bulk carrier. Sister ships BYTOM and MALBORK II were built about the same time.

BYTOM is listed in PZM's fleet as a coaster with a grain capacity of 204,763 cubic feet registered under the Panama flag. [Company website current 2007].

MV KOSCIERZYNA was the last ship built at the Caledon Shipyard though two other projects followed namely a dock gate for Yarrow's yard and a small river ferry TYNE COUNTESS for Swan Hunter's yard at Wallsend.[DM]

Built   1980   **Yard No**   577

Specifications
 2996 Gross tons
 88 x 14.6 x 7.6 metres

Machinery
Diesel 2700BHP Sulzer type 6ZL40/48
6 Cyl 400 Dia 480 Stroke
14 knots

Complement
0 Passengers   23 Crew

Index of Ships included in this book

INDEX OF SHIPS		TABLE 1	
Ship	Type	Year	Page
ABERTAY	LS	1939	60
ABOYNE	SS	1936	43
ACHILLES	MV	1947	94
ACTIVITY	TSMV	1942	68
AIDA	MV	1951	106
ALMERIAN	SS	1956	126
ANCHISES	MV	1946	88
ARBROATH	MV	1935	28
ASCOT	SS	1943	74
ATHELPRINCE	MV	1959	136
ATHELPRINCESS	MV	1959	136
ATHELVICTOR	MV	1940	63
B L NAIRN	PS	1929	20
BACCHUS	SS	1936	38
BAHARISTAN	MV	1959	135
BARON GLENCONNOR	SS	1955	120
BARON KILMARNOCK	MV	1952	114
BAROSSA	SS	1938	50
BARWEN	SS	1939	61
BEACHY	MV	1946	93
BEACONSFIELD	SS	1938	58
BECKENHAM	SS	1937	46
BELLEROPHON	MV	1950	104
BELTANA	SS	1937	42
BENARTY	MV	1962	141
BEXLEY	TSMV	1966	147
BILLITON	SS	1950	111
BLACKHEATH	SS	1936	33
BRALANTA	TSMV	1931	24
BUNDALEER	SS	1939	55
BUNGAREE	SS	1937	41
BYTOM	MV	1980	160
CAEDMON	MV	1973	155
CALEDONIAN MONARCH	SS	1948	99
CALIFORNIAN	SS	1900	3
CANADIAN STAR	MV	1957	128
CARISBROOKE CASTLE	HMS	1943	84
CHARON	MV	1936	37
CITY OF DUNDEE	MV	1961	137
CITY OF HEREFORD	MV	1958	133
CITY OF HULL	MV	1971	152
CITY OF LIVERPOOL	MV	1970	152
CITY OF PERTH	SS	1948	101
CITY OF WINNIPEG	MV	1956	124
CITY OF WORCESTER	MV	1960	137
CLYTONEUS	MV	1948	100
CONSTANCE BOWATER	MV	1958	132
DHT No8	Barge	1961	142
DIOMED	MV	1956	125
DP-ZS-1 Crane	Barge	1974	156
DUNDEE	SS	1933	27
EDDYBEACH	SS	1951	105

INDEX OF SHIPS   TABLE 2

Ship	Type	Year	Page
EDDYREEF	SS	1953	118
ELIZABETH BOWATER	MV	1958	131
EMPIRE ARCHER	SS	1942	71
EMPIRE BARD	SS	1941	72
EMPIRE CANNING	SS	1944	83
EMPIRE CANYON	SS	1943	80
EMPIRE CAPTAIN	SS	1944	78
EMPIRE FAVOUR	SS	1945	82
EMPIRE HEYWOOD	SS	1941	70
EMPIRE KITCHENER	SS	1944	79
EMPIRE LIFE	SS	1945	79
EMPIRE PRINCE	SS	1942	71
EMPIRE RHODES	SS	1941	71
ENGLAND	MV	1947	96
ERNEST BEVIN	MV	1963	143
EUMAEUS	MV	1953	117
FINGAL	SS	1894	1
FORMBY	SS	1914	11
GLAMIS	MV	1936	39
GLENARTNEY	TSMV	1939	54
GLENEARN	MV	1938	47
GLENGYLE	TSMV	1939	52
GOLD RANGER	SS	1941	69
GOLDEN BAY	MV	1979	159
GOLDFINCH	MV	1936	40
GORGON	MV	1933	26
GRIVE	SS	1905	6
HARECRAIG	SS	1936	34
HERON	MV	1937	45
HESPERUS	TSMV	1939	62
IDA LUNDRIGAN	MV	1972	154
IRIS	MV	1976	157
IVERNIA	MV	1964	144
JAMES NEWMAN	MV	1963	143
JOHN BURNS	MV	1963	143
JON RAMSOY	MV	1972	153
JUJUY II	MV	1977	158
KHOEN HOED	SS	1924	16
KIMANIS	TSMV	1951	109
KINTA	SS	1907	7
KOORINGA	SS	1937	51
KOSCIERZYNA	MV	1980	160
KURGAN	SS	1903	4
KYLECLARE	SS	1932	25
LAPLAND	SS	1942	77
LOCH ARKAIG	HMS	1945	86
LOCH LOMOND	HMS	1944	85
LOCH MORE	HMS	1944	85
LOCH TRALAIG	HMS	1945	86
LOUISE BORNHOFEN	MV	1967	149
LYMINGE	MV	1967	148
MACHAON	SS	1916	12
MACHAON	MV	1959	134
MAHENO	MV	1969	150

INDEX OF SHIPS		TABLE 3	
Ship	Type	Year	Page
MALLARD	MV	1936	35
MARAMA	MV	1969	150
MARON	TSMV	1929	21
MEMNON	TSMV	1930	23
MENELAUS	MV	1957	129
MENESTHEUS	MV	1958	129
MODJOKERTO	MV	1946	87
MONARCH	MV	1975	157
MORIALTA	MV	1940	64
NELIUS	SS	1953	113
NESTOR	SS	1952	113
NEWHAM	TSMV	1967	147
NGAHERE	MV	1965	146
NGAKUTA	MV	1962	140
NGAPARA	MV	1965	146
NGATORO	MV	1962	140
NINA BOWATER	MV	1961	138
NORMAN MONARCH	SS	1937	44
NORNA	SS	1909	9
NORWEGIAN	SS	1913	10
PARTHIA	MV	1963	144
PERLIS	MV	1954	123
PHAROS	MV	1955	127
PHILOMEL	SS	1935	31
PLOVER	MV	1936	36
POLE STAR	TSMV	1961	139
PORT ALBANY	MV	1965	145
PORT ANNA	MV	1971	153
PORT HUON	MV	1965	145
PORTSDOWN	PS	1928	18
PRIAM	TSMV	1941	67
RAJAH BROOKE	TSMV	1947	91
RATNAGIRI	SS	1935	29
RHEXENOR	MV	1945	81
ROYAL FUSILIER	SS	1922	15
RUTLAND	SS	1935	30
SALMO	SS	1900	2
SALTA	MV	1977	158
SANDA	MV	1949	107
SCHWEDAGA	MV	1947	95
SCOTLAND	MV	1946	90
SCOTSCRAIG	MV	1951	112
SCOTT	SS	1938	56
SCOTTISH MONARCH	SS	1938	59
SCOTTISH MONARCH	SS	1943	76
SEAFORTH	MV	1938	49
SELANGOR	SS	1903	5
SHEKATIKA	SS	1936	32
ST NINIAN	TSMV	1950	108
STAR OF ASSUAN	MV	1947	98
STENTOR	MV	1945	81
STORAAS	MV	1954	121
SUNNAS	MV	1951	106
SUVARNABHUMI	TSMV	1969	151
SWIFTPOOL	MV	1954	119

INDEX OF SHIPS		TABLE 4	
Ship	**Type**	**Year**	**Page**
SZECHUEN	MV	1946	89
TABOR	MV	1951	110
TAMBUA	SS	1938	57
TANIMBAR	MV	1930	22
TANTALUS	MV	1922	14
TARKWA	MV	1943	75
TELEMACHUS	MV	1943	73
TEMPLEHALL	MV	1954	116
TEMPLEMAIN	MV	1958	130
TERBORCH	SS	1944	79
THESEUS	SS	1955	122
TOTTENHAM	SS	1940	65
TOWARD	TSMV	1946	92
TRIAD	SS	1909	8
TUSKAR	SS	1920	13
TWICKENHAM	SS	1940	66
TEDDINGTON	SS	1941	66
TEMPLEHALL	MV	1954	116
WALLASEY	SS	1927	17
WANSTEAD	MV	1949	103
WATFORD	SS	1928	19
WOKINGHAM	MV	1953	115
WOODLAND	SS	1948	102
WOOLWICH	MV	1955	115